FROM HERE TO ETERNITY

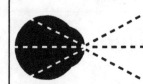

This Large Print Book carries the
Seal of Approval of N.A.V.H.

FROM HERE TO ETERNITY

TRAVELING THE WORLD TO FIND THE GOOD DEATH

CAITLIN DOUGHTY

Illustrations by Landis Blair

THORNDIKE PRESS
A part of Gale, a Cengage Company

GALE
A Cengage Company

Farmington Hills, Mich • San Francisco • New York • Waterville, Maine
Meriden, Conn • Mason, Ohio • Chicago

Copyright © 2017 by Caitlin Doughty.
Thorndike Press, a part of Gale, a Cengage Company.

ALL RIGHTS RESERVED
Thorndike Press® Large Print Popular and Narrative Nonfiction.
The text of this Large Print edition is unabridged.
Other aspects of the book may vary from the original edition.
Set in 16 pt. Plantin.

LIBRARY OF CONGRESS CIP DATA ON FILE.
CATALOGUING IN PUBLICATION FOR THIS BOOK
IS AVAILABLE FROM THE LIBRARY OF CONGRESS

ISBN-13: 978-1-4328-4853-8 (hardcover)

Published in 2018 by arrangement with W.W. Norton & Company, Inc.

Printed in Mexico
1 2 3 4 5 6 7 22 21 20 19 18

FOR MOM & DAD —
& all parents who let the weird kids
be weird.

Adults who are racked with death anxiety are not odd birds who have contracted some exotic disease, but men and women whose family and culture have failed to knit the proper protective clothing for them to withstand the icy chill of mortality.

— IRVIN YALOM, PSYCHIATRIST

CONTENTS

CONTENTS

AUTHOR'S NOTE

From Here to Eternity is a work of nonfiction. I have changed a small number of names and descriptive details.

INTRODUCTION

The phone rang and my heart raced.

The first few months after I opened my funeral home, a ringing phone qualified as a thrilling event. We didn't get many calls. "What if . . . what if someone *died*?" I'd gasp. (Well yes, dear, it's a funeral home — that would be the point.)

The voice on the other end was a hospice nurse. She had declared Josephine dead ten minutes ago; the body was still warm to the touch. The nurse sat at the dead woman's bedside, having an argument with Josephine's daughter. The daughter had chosen to call my funeral home because she didn't want her mother whisked away the second she took her final breath. She wanted to keep Mom's body at home.

"Can she do that?"

"Of course she can," I replied. "In fact, we encourage it."

"That's not illegal?" the nurse asked skeptically.

"It's not illegal."

"Usually we call the funeral home and they pick up the body within the hour."

"The daughter is in control of her body. Not the hospice, not a hospital or nursing home, definitely not the funeral home."

"Well, okay, if you're sure."

"I'm sure," I said. "Please tell Josephine's daughter she can call us back later this evening, or tomorrow morning if she'd prefer! Whenever she's ready."

We picked up Josephine at 8 p.m., six hours after her death. The next day her daughter sent us a video she shot on her cellphone. In the thirty-second clip, the dead woman lies in bed, dressed in her favorite sweater and scarf. Candles flicker on the dresser beside the bed, and the body is covered in flower petals.

Even in the grainy cellphone footage, you could tell that Josephine looked radiant her last night on Earth. Her daughter felt genuine pride in her accomplishment. Her mother had always taken care of her, and now she was taking care of her mother.

Not everyone in my industry is supportive of the way I run my funeral home. Some believe a dead body must be embalmed to be safe (untrue) and that a body should be handled only by licensed professionals (also untrue). The dissenters imagine that younger, progressive morticians are "starting to make our profession look like a joke" and wonder if "circus is the right word for what funeral service is becoming." One gentleman promised, "The day the funeral business turns into three-day visitations at the house of an un-embalmed body, I'm done!"

In America, where I live, death has been big business since the turn of the twentieth century. A century has proven the perfect amount of time for its citizens to forget what funerals once were: family- and community-run affairs. In the nineteenth century no one would have questioned Josephine's daughter preparing her mother's body — it would have seemed strange if she *didn't*. No one would have questioned a wife washing and dressing the body of her husband or a father carrying his son to the grave in a homemade coffin. In an impressively short time, America's funeral industry has become more expensive, more corporate, and more bureaucratic than any other funeral industry on Earth. If we can be called best at anything, it would be at keeping our grieving families separated from their dead.

Five years ago, when my funeral home (and this book) was still a gleam in my eye, I rented a hut on a rural lagoon in Belize. At that time I lived the glamorous life of a crematory worker and body transport driver — the hut had to be *very* inexpensive. It had neither cellphone service nor Wi-Fi. The lagoon was nine miles from the nearest town, reachable only by four-wheel drive. The driver was the caretaker of the property, a thirty-year-old Belizean man named Luciano.

To give you a sense of Luciano, he was shadowed everywhere by his pack of loyal, if somewhat emaciated, dogs. When the hut was unoccupied, he would head into the Belizean bush for days at a time, wearing flip-flops, carrying his machete, followed by the dogs. He hunted deer, tapir, and armadillo, and when he caught one he would kill it, flay it, and eat its heart out of its chest.

Luciano asked me what I did for a living. When I told him I worked with the dead, at a crematory, he sat up in his hammock. "You burn them?" he asked. "You barbecue people?"

I considered this description. "Well, the machine is hotter than that. It gets over 1,800 degrees, so you blast right through the 'barbecue' stage. But pretty much, yes."

When someone died in Luciano's community, the family would bring the body home for a full-day wake. Belize has a diverse population, sandwiched between Caribbean and Latin American influences, with English as the national language. Luciano identified as a mestizo — a descendant of the indigenous Maya and the Spanish colonizers.

Luciano's grandfather was his community's death attendant, the guy a local family would call to prepare a body. When he arrived, sometimes the body would be in rigor mortis, the muscles rendered so stiff it was a challenge to dress and bathe the corpse. According to Luciano, if that were the case, his grandfather would talk to the body.

"Look, you want to look good in heaven? I can't dress you if you want to be hard."

"So your grandfather would *talk* the corpse out of rigor mortis?" I asked.

"Well, you also had to rub a little rum on it to make it loosen up. But yeah, he would just talk to the body," he replied.

After convincing the body to loosen up, his grandfather would flip it over on its stomach and press out any purge or gas from decomposition. Kind of like burping a baby — burp *it* before it burps *on you.*

"Is that your job in America, too?" he

17

wondered, gazing out over the lagoon.

Of course, the larger cities in Belize have funeral homes that adopted the American business models, upselling families on mahogany caskets and marble headstones. The same push toward modernity goes for Belizean hospitals, which may require that an autopsy be performed, whether the family wants the procedure or not. Luciano's grandmother, before she died, refused to be cut open. "That's why we thieved her body from the hospital," Luciano told me.

"I'm sorry, what?"

I had heard correctly: they stole her body from the hospital. Just wrapped it in a sheet and took it. "What was the hospital going to do to us?" Luciano asked.

He has a similar story about his friend, who drowned in this very lagoon. Luciano hadn't bothered to call the authorities to report the drowning. "He was dead, what did they have to do with it?"

When he dies, Luciano would like to be buried in a simple hole, shrouded with an animal skin, with leaves lining the walls of the grave. He plans on designing the animal shroud himself.

He explained that he talks about death "all the time" with his friends. They ask each other, "Hey, what you want when you die?"

Luciano asked, "Don't people say that where you come from?"

It was hard to explain that, no, for the most part, they really don't.

One of the chief questions in my work has always been why my own culture is so squeamish around death. Why do we refuse to have these conversations, asking our family and friends what they want done with their body when they die? Our avoidance is self-defeating. By dodging the talk about our inevitable end, we put both our pocketbooks and our ability to mourn at risk.

I believed that if I could witness firsthand how death is handled in other cultures, I might be able to demonstrate that there is no one prescribed way to "do" or understand death. In the last several years I have traveled to observe death rituals as they are practiced around the world — in Australia, England, Germany, Spain, Italy, Indonesia, Mexico, Bolivia, Japan, and throughout the U.S. There is much to learn from the cremation pyres of India and the whimsical coffins of Ghana, but the places I chose to visit have tales equally spectacular and less often told. I hope that what I found might help us reclaim meaning and tradition in our own communities. Such reclamation is important to me as a funeral home owner, but more so as a daughter and a friend.

The Greek historian Herodotus, writing over two thousand years ago, produced one of the first descriptions of one culture getting worked up over the death rituals of another. In the story, the ruler of the Persian Empire summons a group of Greeks before him. Since they cremate their dead, the king wonders, "What would [it] take [for them] to eat their dead fathers?" The Greeks balk at this question, explaining that no price in the world would be high enough to turn them into cannibals. Next, the king summons a group of Callatians, known for eating the bodies of their dead. He asks, "What price would make them burn their dead fathers with fire?" The Callatians beg him not to mention "such horrors!"

That attitude — revulsion at the way other groups handle their dead — has endured through millennia. If you have ever come within 500 feet of a modern funeral home, you know that morticians *love* the following quote, attributed to William Gladstone, a nineteenth-century British prime minister:

Show me the manner in which a nation

cares for its dead and I will measure with mathematical exactness the tender mercies of its people, their respect for the laws of the land and their loyalty to high ideals.

They etch the quote onto wall plaques and feature it prominently on their websites alongside American flag GIFs and muzak tracks of "Amazing Grace." Unfortunately, Gladstone never supplied the equation that would allow us to determine, with his promised "mathematical exactness," that one particular method of handling the dead is 79.9 percent barbaric while another is 62.4 percent dignified.

(In fact, Gladstone may have never even produced this quote at all. It is first recorded as appearing in the March 1938 issue of *The American Cemetery,* in an article called "Successful Cemetery Advertising." I can't prove Gladstone didn't say it, but one prominent Gladstone scholar told me he had never come across the quote. The furthest he would go was to say it "sounded like something he could have said.")

Even if we recognize the benefits of another culture's ritual, we often allow bias to undermine those feelings of acceptance. In 1636, two thousand indigenous Wendat people gathered around a communal burial pit on the shores of what is now Lake Huron, Canada. The grave measured six feet deep and twenty-four feet across, and was designed to hold the bones of seven hundred individuals.

For the bones, the burial pit was not their first stop after death. When the bones were still fresh corpses, they were wrapped in beaver-skin robes and placed on wooden scaffolds ten feet off the ground. Every decade or so, the scattered Huron–Wendat communities would gather their remains for the communal burial, known as the Feast of the Dead. In preparation, the bodies were brought down from the scaffolds. Family members, mostly women, were tasked with scraping the bones clean of any lingering flesh.

How difficult it was to clean the bones varied according to how long the person had been dead. Some bodies had decomposed, and only dried, paper-thin skin still clung to the skeleton. Other bodies were preserved and near mummified, requiring the desiccated flesh to be pulled off in strips and burned. The most challenging bodies belonged to the recently deceased, still swarming with maggots.

This cleaning ritual was witnessed and recorded by Jean de Brébeuf, a Catholic

missionary from France. Instead of reacting with horror, he wrote with great admiration of the intimate way the families treated the bodies. In one such case, Brébeuf observed a family unwrap a corpse oozing with decomposition. The family, undaunted, plunged in to clean the bones and rewrap them in a new beaver robe. Brébeuf asked if this was not "a noble example to inspire Christians." He expressed similar admiration when it came to the ceremony at the burial pit. When the bodies were covered over with sand and bark, he found it "heartening to see" such "works of mercy" take place.

In that moment, standing at the edge of the pit, I'm sure Brébeuf was moved by the death rituals of the Wendat people. But it did not change his final, fervent hope: that all of their customs and ceremonies would be obliterated and replaced with Christian ceremonies, so they could be "sacred" as opposed to "foolish and useless."

It should be stated that the indigenous people of Canada were not altogether open-minded toward the alternative rituals that missionary de Brébeuf offered. Historian Erik Seeman wrote that the First Nations and Europeans often discovered "chilling perversions" about each other. How were the Wendats expected to believe the French Catholics had noble aims, when they freely admitted to cannibalism, bragging that they consumed flesh and blood (of their own God no less) in a practice called Communion?

Since religion is the source of many death rituals, often we invoke belief to denigrate the practices of others. As recently as 1965, James W. Fraser wrote in *Cremation: Is It Christian?* (spoiler: no) that to cremate was "a barbarous act" and "an aid to crime." To a decent Christian, it is "repulsive to think of the body of a friend being treated like a beef roast in the oven, with all its running fats and sizzling tissues."

I have come to believe that the merits of a death custom are not based on mathematics (e.g., 36.7 percent a "barbarous act"), but on emotions, a belief in the unique nobility of one's own culture. That is to say, we consider death rituals savage only when they don't match our own.

On my last day in Belize, Luciano took me to the cemetery that houses his grandparents (including the stolen grandmother). The cemetery was filled with above-ground concrete graves, some well-tended, some fallen into disrepair. One cross, knocked

over into the weeds, was wrapped in a pair of ladies' underwear. Someone had taken black spray paint and crudely painted "Gaza Earth" and "Repent All Man" on a pair of graves.

Back in the far corner, under a tree, his grandparents' caskets lay stacked one on top of the other, enclosed in one of the concrete-covered graves. "My grandmother, she didn't want all this cement. She wanted just a hole in the ground, dust to dust. But, you know . . ."

Luciano lovingly swept the dead leaves off the top of the grave.

What struck me was how Luciano had been present for every step of his grandmother's death. From stealing her body from the hospital, to holding a wake where the family drank rum and played *ranchera* music (Grandma's favorite), to tending her grave years later.

Contrast that with the Western funeral industry, where mourners must navigate purposeful obfuscations after every loss. Most people could not tell you what chemicals are pumped into their mother during an embalming procedure (answer: some combination of formaldehyde, methanol, ethanol, and phenol), or why they are required to purchase a $3,000 stainless steel vault at the cemetery (answer: so the groundskeeping staff has an easier time mowing the grass). In 2017, an NPR investigation into funeral homes "found a confusing, unhelpful system that seems designed

to be impenetrable by average consumers, who must make costly decisions at a time of grief and financial stress."

We need to reform our funeral industry, introducing new practices that aren't so profit-oriented, and that do more to include the family. But we cannot begin to reform — or even question! — our death systems when we act like little Jean de Brébeufs, falsely convinced we have it right while all these "other people" are disrespectful and barbarous.

This dismissive attitude can be found in places you'd never expect. Lonely Planet, the largest guidebook publisher in the world, included the idyllic Trunyan cemetery in their book on visiting Bali. In Trunyan, the villagers weave bamboo cages for their dead to decompose in, and then stack the skulls and bones out in the lush green landscape. Lonely Planet, instead of explaining the meaning behind these ancient customs, advised wise travelers to "skip the ghoulish spectacle."

Cannibalizing your dear old dad like the Callatians may never be for you. It's not for me, either; I'm a vegetarian (kidding, Dad). Still, it is demonstrably wrong to claim that the West has death rituals that are superior to those of the rest of the world. What's more, due to the corporatization and commercialization of deathcare, we have fallen behind the rest of the world when it comes to proximity, intimacy, and ritual around death.

The good news: we are not beholden to our distance from and shame around death. The first step to fixing the problem is to show up, to be present and engaged. In large, modern cities like Tokyo and Barcelona, I saw families show up to spend the day with the body and stay to witness the cremation. In Mexico, I saw families visit the cemetery to leave offerings years after the death occurred, ensuring that no one is forgotten.

Many of the rituals in this book will be very different from your own, but I hope you will see the beauty in that difference. You may be someone who experiences real fear and anxiety around death, but you are here. Just like the people you are about to meet, you have shown up.

COLORADO: CRESTONE

One afternoon in August I received the email I had been waiting for.

Caitlin,
Laura, a very dear member of our community was found dead early this morning: she had a history of heart problems and had just entered her 75th year. Don't know where you are, but you're welcome to join us.

Stephanie

Laura's death was unexpected. On Sunday night, she danced with abandon at a local music festival. On Monday morning, she lay dead on her kitchen floor. On Thursday morning, her family would gather to cremate her, and I would be there.

The cremation was scheduled to start promptly at 7 a.m., just as the sun broke through the blue light of dawn. The mourners began to stream in after 6:30. A truck pulled up, driven by Laura's son, bearing her body wrapped in a coral-colored shroud. There had been a rumor that her horse, Bebe, would be making an appearance, but at the last minute the family decided the crowd and the fire would be too much for Bebe's constitution. The announcement came that the horse was "regretfully unable to attend."

Laura's family pulled her body from the pickup and carried her on a cloth stretcher through the field of black-eyed susans, up the slight incline toward the pyre. A gong rang through the air. As I walked from the parking area up the sandy path, a beaming volunteer handed me a freshly cut bough of juniper.

Laura was laid out on a metal grate atop two parallel slabs of smooth white concrete, under the expansive dome of Colorado sky. I had come to visit the empty pyre twice before, but its purpose became more sober and clear with the presence of a body. One by one, mourners stepped forward to lay a juniper bough on Laura's body. As the only person present who hadn't known her, I hesitated to deposit my juniper — call it funereal awkwardness. But I couldn't very well hang on to my bough (too obvious) or stuff it into my backpack (tacky) so I walked forward and rested it on the shroud.

Laura's family, including a young boy of eight or nine, circled her pyre stacking piñon pine and spruce logs, selected because they burn with heightened intensity. Laura's partner and her adult son waited at the corners with lit torches. A signal was given, and they came together to set Laura aflame, just as the sun peered above the horizon.

As her body caught fire, white smoke swirled about in tiny cyclones, twisting upward and disappearing into morning sky.

The smell called to mind a passage from Edward Abbey:

> The fire. The odor of burning juniper is the sweetest fragrance on the face of the earth, in my honest judgment; I doubt if all the smoking censers of Dante's paradise could equal it. One breath of juniper smoke, like the perfume of sagebrush after rain, evokes in magical catalysis, like certain music, the space and light and clarity and piercing strangeness of the American West. Long may it burn.

After a few minutes the whirlwinds dispersed, and glowing red flames danced in their place. The fire gathered strength,

shooting up six feet high. The mourners, all 130 of them, ringed the pyre in silence. The only sound was the pop of flaming wood, as if one by one Laura's memories were diffusing into the ether.

Cremation, in the form they practice it in the tiny town of Crestone, Colorado, has been around for tens of thousands of years. The ancient Greeks, Romans, and Hindus were most famous for employing the modest alchemy of fire to consume the flesh and liberate the soul. But cremation itself goes back even further.

In the late 1960s, in the remote Australian Outback, a young geologist discovered the cremated bones of an adult woman. He estimated the bones might be up to 20,000 years old. In fact, further study revealed that they were 42,000 years old, antedating the supposed arrival of the Aboriginal people in Australia by some 22,000 years. The woman would have lived in a verdant landscape filled with giant creatures (kangaroos, wombats, other rodents of unusual size). For food she collected fish, seeds, and the eggs of enormous emus. When she died, the woman, now known as Mungo Lady, was cremated by her community. After the cremation, her bones were crushed and then burned again in a second cremation. They were ritually covered with red ocher before being buried in the ground, where they lay resting for 42,000 years.

Speaking of Australia (this transition will pay off, I promise), ten minutes into Laura's cremation, one of the fire-tenders picked up a didgeridoo and signaled a gentleman holding a wooden flute to join her.

I braced myself. The didgeridoo is a ludicrous instrument for an American funeral. But the combination of the didgeridoo's all-encompassing drone and the flute's lament was haunting, soothing the crowd as they stared deeper into the flames.

And so it goes: another American small town, another grieving community gathered around the pyre. Except, obviously, not. Crestone's pyre is the only community open-air pyre in America and, in fact, in the Western world.*

Cremations in Crestone didn't always employ such stirring rituals. Before the processions at dawn and the didgeridoos and the well-organized juniper dispersers, there were Stephanie, Paul, and their Porta-Pyre.

* There is one other pyre, a private pyre, at the Shambala Mountain Center, a Buddhist retreat in northern Colorado.

"We were the Porta-Pyre people," Stephanie Gaines explained matter-of-factly. She describes herself as a hyper-engaged Buddhist. "I'm a power Aries," she added, "a triple Aries — my Sun, Moon, and ascendant." At seventy-two, she rules Crestone's pyre operation with logistics, charm, and a white-banged bob.

Stephanie and Paul Kloppenberg, an equally enchanting character with a thick Dutch accent, kept the pyre mobile, moving it from place to place, cremating on private property, swooping in and out before the county could stop them. They ran this portable operation for seven cremations.

"We'd just come set it up at the end of your cul de sac," Paul said.

The Porta-Pyre was a low-tech system, built from cinderblocks with a grate laid on top. The intense heat would cause the grate to warp and sag after every cremation. "We had to drive a truck over the top of it to get it flat again," Stephanie said. "It seems crazy, looking back now," she added, amused but not apologetic.

In 2006, the pair began searching for a more permanent location for the pyre. Crestone seemed like the perfect place, the very definition of rural, four hours south of Denver, population 137 people (1,400 in the surrounding areas). This gives Crestone a libertarian, "government outta my business" sort of edge. Weed is legal there, as are brothels. (Not that there are any brothels in operation, but there *could* be.)

The town attracts a mélange of spiritual seekers. People come from all over the world to meditate there, the Dalai Lama included. Flyers at the natural foods store advertise Qigong instructors, shadow wisdom teachers, retreats for children to "awaken their natural genius," retreats for North African dance classes, and something called the "Enchanted Forest Sacred Space." Crestone's residents include hippies and trustafarians, but many who live here are serious lifelong practitioners: Buddhists, Sufis, and Carmelite nuns. Laura herself had spent decades as a devotee of the Indian philosopher Sri Aurobindo.

Paul and Stephanie's first proposal for the permanent pyre location was squelched when landowners downwind of the site — "smokers, mind you," Paul pointed out — developed a serious case of "not in my backyard." They were "curmudgeons," Stephanie said, uninterested in evidence showing no threat of wildfires, unpleasant smells, mercury poisoning, or particulate matter. The smokers wrote letters to the county board and the Environmental Protection Agency.

To fight them, the Porta-Pyre crew went legit. They created a nonprofit, the Crestone End of Life Project. They filed motion after motion, collected four hundred signatures (almost a third of the surrounding area), and amassed huge binders full of legal documents and scientific papers. They even visited the residents of Crestone one by one and listened to their concerns.

At first, they met strong resistance. One man in the anti-pyre camp termed the group "Neighbors Burning Neighbors." When Paul and Stephanie suggested (as a joke) sponsoring a float in the local parade, a family came forward protesting that it was "horribly disrespectful" to feature a float decorated with papier-mâché flames.

"Folks in the town even worried the pyre would bring too much traffic," Stephanie said. "Keep in mind that for Crestone, six cars is traffic."

Paul explained, "There's a lot of fear. 'What about air pollution? Is it not morbid? Death stuff gives me the creeps.' You have to stay patient, listen to what they're asking for."

Paul and Stephanie kept going, in spite of the overwhelming legal hurdles, because the idea of the pyre inspired the community. (Recall that the residents were so excited about the chance to be cremated on a pyre that they were summoning Paul and Stephanie to set up a cinderblock grill in their driveways.) "How many people provide a service that actually resonates with other people?" Stephanie asked. "If it's not resonating, forget it. It was that resonance that fed me."

They at last found their pyre a stable home: outside of town, a few hundred yards off the main road. The land was donated by Dragon Mountain Temple, a Zen Buddhist group. They don't keep the pyre hidden. As you drive into town there is a metal sign with a single flame reading "PYRE." The sign was handmade by a local potato farmer (also the coroner), and stands as an obvious landmark. The pyre itself sits on a bed of sand, ringed with a bamboo wall that swoops and curves like calligraphy. Over fifty people have been cremated there, including (dramatic twist) the "Neighbors Burning Neighbors" guy, who had a change of heart prior to his death.

Three days before Laura's cremation, volunteers from the Crestone End of Life Project came to her home. They prepared her body, helped her friends wash her, and laid her out on a cooling blanket to slow down any decomposition. They dressed her in natural fabrics — synthetics like polyester don't perform well on the pyre.

The organization will assist a family with its postmortem logistics regardless of finances. The family doesn't have to choose open-air cremation, either. The volunteers at Crestone End of Life are prepared to help whether the family chooses a conventional (embalmed) burial, a natural (no vault or embalming) burial, or a cremation at the funeral home several towns over. Paul referred to the last option as "commercial cremation."

Stephanie interrupted, "Paul, you're supposed to call it *conventional* cremation."

"No," I argued, "commercial cremation sounds right."

Crestone was inspiring to me as a practitioner — which is why I kept returning — but there was also a touch of melancholy (that bordered on jealousy). They had this glorious pyre under the blue sky, while I had to take my families to a loud, dusty crematory in a warehouse on the outskirts of town. I'd even promise to invite the didgeridoo player if I could have access to such a spectacular cremation facility for my funeral home.

Industrial, furnace cremation was first proposed in Europe in the late nineteenth century. In 1869, a group of medical experts gathered in Florence, Italy, to denounce burial as unhygienic and advocate a switch to cremation. Almost simultaneously, the pro-cremation movement jumped the pond to America, led by reformers such as the absurdly named Reverend Octavius B. Frothingham, who believed it was better for the dead body to transform into "white ashes" than a "mass of corruption." (My next drone folk album will be called *The Cremation Reforms of Octavius B. Frothingham.*)

The first body to undergo a "modern, scientific" cremation in America was that of Baron Joseph Henry Louis Charles De Palm. (Scratch that, the drone folk album is now *The Burning of Baron De Palm.*) The good Baron, a penniless Austrian nobleman, whom the *New York Tribune* called "principally famous as a corpse" (literal and figurative burn), died in May 1876.

His cremation was scheduled for December, six months after his death. In the interim his corpse was injected with arsenic, and when arsenic was deemed too weak to prevent rot, his organs were pulled from his body and his skin was covered with clay and carbolic acid by a local undertaker. On the train journey from New York to Pennsylvania (where he would be cremated), his mummified corpse briefly went missing in the baggage car, launching what historian Stephen Prothero called "a macabre game of hide-and-seek."

The crematory for this inaugural event was built on a physician's estate in Pennsylvania. It contained a coal-fired furnace that was supposed to cremate the body without the flames ever having to touch it — the heat alone would disintegrate the corpse. Even though the physician said the cremation would be "a strictly scientific and sanitary experiment," De Palm's body was still sprinkled with spices and placed on a bed of roses, palms, primroses, and evergreens. When the body first went into the furnace, observers reported a distinct smell of burning flesh, but the smell soon gave way to the aromas of flower and spice. After an hour in the furnace, De Palm's body began to glow with a rose mist. The glow turned gold, and finally shone transparent red. After two and half hours, the body had disintegrated into bone and ash. Newspapermen and reviewers at the scene declared that the experiment had resulted in "the first careful and inodorous baking of a human being in an oven."

From there, cremation machines only grew larger, faster, and more efficient. Almost 150 years later, cremation has reached record heights in popularity (for the first time, in 2017, more Americans will be cremated than buried). But the aesthetics and ritual surrounding the process have hardly changed. Our cremation machines still resemble the models introduced in the 1870s — 24,000-pound behemoths of steel, brick, and concrete. They gobble thousands of dollars' worth of natural gas a month, spewing carbon monoxide, soot, sulfur dioxide, and highly toxic mercury (from dental fillings) into the atmosphere.

Most crematories, especially in larger cities, are relegated to industrial zones, tucked inside nondescript warehouses. Of the three crematories I have worked at in my nine years in the funeral industry, one was across from the *Los Angeles Times* distribution warehouse, where freight trucks rumbled out at all hours, one was behind a "Structural and Termite" warehouse (who knows what they do there), and one was next door to a junkyard where cars were torn apart for scrap metal.

One might find a crematory located on the grounds of a cemetery, but those facili-

ties are most often hidden within the cemetery's maintenance buildings, meaning mourners who wish to attend the cremation must navigate John Deere mowers and piles of rotting flower wreaths collected from the graves.

Some crematories are styled as "celebration of life facilities" or "cremation tribute centers." Families are kept behind glass windows in air-conditioned rooms, watching as the body disappears into a small metal door in the wall. The machine concealed behind the wall is the same industrial oven found in the warehouses, but the family cannot see the wizard behind the curtain. The camouflage removes the family further from the reality of death and of the clunky, environmentally inefficient machines. For the privilege of taking mom to a "cremation tribute center," the price may rise above $5,000.

I'm not arguing that a switch to open-air cremation would resolve all of these issues. In countries where pyre cremation is the norm, such as India and Nepal, the many millions of cremations every year burn 50 million-plus trees and release carbon aerosols into the atmosphere. After carbon dioxide, carbon aerosols are the second leading man-made cause of climate change.

But the Crestone model comes close. The nonprofit has received several calls from reformers in India wanting to adopt the structure and methods of their pyre — raised high off the ground to use less wood and release less damaging pollution. If reform is possible for this ancient method, inextricably tied to religion and country, then reform is possible for the modern, industrial cremation machines as well.

Laura had lived in Crestone for years, and it seemed as if the whole town had come to the pyre that morning. Her son, Jason, spoke the first words, his gaze focused on the flames. "Mom, thank you for the love," he said, his voice cracking. "Don't worry about us now, fly and be free."

As the fire continued to burn, a woman came forward to describe her own arrival in Crestone eleven years prior. When she moved to town, she had been suffering from years of chronic illness. "I moved to Crestone to find joy. I thought it was the clouds and the open sky that healed me, but I think it really was Laura."

"We're all just human beings," another of her friends added. "We all have faults. But Laura, I didn't see no faults about her."

The flames had made quick work of Laura's coral shroud. As mourners spoke, the flames jumped to her exposed flesh and the layers of soft tissue. The fire dehydrated the tissue, the majority of which was water, which shriveled and withered away. This exposed her internal organs, next to succumb to the flames.

This would be a macabre spectacle for the uninitiated, but the nonprofit volunteers were vigilant in concealing the pyre's inner workings from the crowd. They moved with grace and expertise, ensuring there was no odor, no threat of a rogue head or charred arm popping into view. "We're not trying to hide the body from people," Stephanie explained, "but the cremations are often open to the entire community, and you never know who is going to be there, and how they are going to respond to the intensity of feeling the pyre can provoke. People imagine themselves lying on that pyre one day."

As the ceremony proceeded, the volunteers crept imperceptibly around the pyre, adding wood. Over the course of the cremation, the nonprofit burned one-third of a cord of wood: 42.6 cubic feet.

As the flames burned on, they reached Laura's bones. The knees, heels, and facial bones were first. It took longer for the fire to reach her pelvis and arm and leg bones. The water evaporated from her skeleton, followed by the organic material. The color of her bones transformed from white, to grey, to black, and then back to white once more. The weight of the logs pressed Laura's bones through the metal grate to the ground below.

One of the fire-tenders pulled out a long metal pole, sending it into the fire. The pole pushed through the space where Laura's head had been, but the skull had vanished.

I had been told that each cremation at

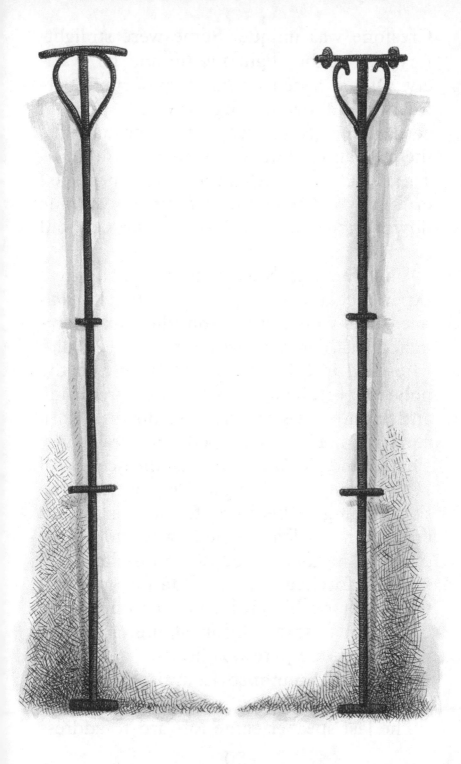

Crestone was unique. Some were straight-forward, of the "light me up and go" variety. Others lasted hours, as mourners performed elaborate religious and spiritual ceremonies. Some were more casual, like the cremation of the young man who wanted a half gallon of tequila and a joint placed on his pyre. "Well, I can tell you everyone downwind enjoyed it," one volunteer told me.

What remains consistent is that the pyre experience, for those present, is transformative. The youngest person they have cremated was Travis, just twenty-two years old, who died in a car crash. According to the police report, he and his friends were drunk and high, speeding too fast down a dark rural road. The car flipped, and Travis was ejected and declared dead at the scene. All of the young people from Crestone and the surrounding towns came to take part in his cremation. As Travis's body was laid on the pyre, his mother pulled down his shroud to kiss his forehead. Travis's father grabbed the driver by his face and, in front of the community, said, "Look at me, I forgive you." Then the pyre was lit.

About an hour into Laura's cremation, the pall of grief had lifted from the circle.

The last speaker came forward to address

the crowd in a way that would have been inappropriate just ninety minutes earlier. "Everything you all said about how Laura was a wonderful person, that's true. But in my mind, she'll always be one of the wild crones. A partier. I'd like to give her a howl."

"Ooooooooooooooooooooooooo," she bellowed, with the crowd joining in around her. Even I, who had just recently been too timid to drop my juniper bough on the pyre, let out a tentative howl.

By 9:30 that morning, only Stephanie and I (and what remained of Laura) were left at the pyre, sitting on a carved wooden bench. Just three logs remained among the embers, in their gentle, end-stage burn. An infrared gun from the fire department measured these embers at over 1,250 degrees.

Stephanie is often the first to arrive and the last to leave the cremation site. "I like the silence," she said.

Stephanie stayed still for a few minutes, and then suddenly she was on her feet again. She picked up a piece of metal grating and examined it. "This is Paul's new spark protector design. It's supposed to keep the ashes contained on a windy night. Chunks of wood can't get out, but what about sparks from the embers?"

51

Within a couple of minutes, Stephanie was on the phone with the fire department to arrange spark protector tests and an inspection. Her boundless energy didn't allow her to remain idle for long. I wondered how she had been able to summon the years of patience required to make this pyre a reality. "It was exhausting, waiting for the community to accept us. It was so hard for me to not drag people in."

The longer I spent in Crestone, the more it seemed like a morbid Mayberry. The nonprofit hosts get-togethers for locals to make sure their end-of-life paperwork is in order. People stop Stephanie in the post office to say, "I'm glad you're here, I'm coming to the next meeting to fill out my advance directive." People in Crestone just *know* what to do when someone dies. The volunteers who go into homes to prepare the bodies told me that families have started to tell them, "Oh, thanks for coming but it's okay, we can take it from here."

Even the corpses have a small-town feel. One woman decided she wanted to be buried in Crestone's natural burial ground (the first in the state). When she died, her daughters drove her body down from Denver in the back of a truck in a Rubbermaid container filled with ice.

"We didn't have anywhere to put the woman until burial," Stephanie said, "so we decided to keep her overnight in the town museum."

The daughters liked that idea. "Mom was such a history buff, she would have been into that."

The natural burial ground is open to anyone, but the pyre is restricted to those living in the community. The nonprofit receives calls from all over the country, from Hindus, Buddhists, Native Americans, and general pyre enthusiasts who want their bodies sent to Crestone after they die. As a small volunteer operation, they just don't have the ability or manpower to handle out-of-town corpses (even if they did, the local commissioner only allows them to serve the surrounding county). Having to decline is difficult for both sides.

The only time they made an exception was when a hiker from Georgia, missing for nine months and the subject of a massive search, was found. Well, a portion of him was found — his spine, his hip, and a leg. They agreed to do the cremation, deciding that he had "established his residency post-mortem."

The pyre funeral is so appealing that some people have even bought land in Crestone just to qualify for an open-air cremation. A forty-two-year-old woman dying of cervical cancer obtained a small plot of land, and when she died her twelve-year-old daughter helped prepare her body for the pyre.

This existential longing for the pyre's fiery embrace is common worldwide. In India, family members transport dead bodies to a row of cremation pyres along the banks of the Ganges River. When a father dies, his pyre will be lit by his eldest son. As the flames grow hotter, his flesh bubbles and

burns away. At just the right time, a wooden staff is brought forth and used to crack open the dead man's skull. At that moment, it is believed the man's soul is released.

A son, describing the cremations of his parents, wrote that "before [breaking the skull], you shiver — for this person was alive just a few hours back — but once you hit the skull, you know what burns in front of you is after all just a body. All attachments are gone." The soul is set free, as an Indian spiritual song intones over a loudspeaker: "Death, you think you have defeated us, but we sing the song of burning firewood."

Pittu Laugani, a Hindu living in the West, explains the pain of witnessing a commercial, industrialized cremation. Instead of placing the body onto the wood of the pyre, mourners watch the coffin "slide off on an electrically operated carousel and drop into a concealed hole." Locked away in the steel and brick-lined chamber, when the skull cracks open, the man's soul will be imprisoned in the machine, forced to mingle with the thousands of other souls the machine has trapped. It will be an *akal mrtya,* a bad death. For the family, the whole process "can be an unnerving and even grotesque experience."

Davender Ghai, a Hindu activist, has

fought Newcastle City Council in England for years to legalize pyres like the one in Crestone. Ghai won the court battle, and open-air pyres may soon be a reality in the U.K. He explained that "being bundled into a box and incinerated in a furnace is not my idea of dignity, much less the performance of an ancient sacrament."

It would be simple to allow open-air pyres in any community that wanted them. Yet government cemetery and funeral boards put up enormous resistance to the idea. Like the curmudgeonly neighbors in Crestone, they argue that outdoor pyres would prove too hard to control, and that they would impact air quality and the environment in unknown ways. Crestone has proven that open-air pyres can be inspected for safety compliance just like any industrial crematory. Environmental agencies can run tests to determine the environmental impact, and regulate accordingly. So why do these local governments continue to resist?

The answer is as bleak as it is obvious: money. The average American funeral costs $8,000 to $10,000 — not including the burial plot and cemetery costs. A Crestone End of Life funeral costs $500, technically a donation "to cover wood, fire department presence, stretcher, and land use." To put this cost in perspective, that's roughly 5 percent of the price of a traditional American funeral. If you don't have the money but are a member of the community, the nonprofit will even forgo its fee. Ghai promises a similar model for pyre cremations in the U.K. He plans to charge £900, but says "we will do this as a charity, for free. They only need to find the land."

In the twenty-first century, removing money and profit from death is almost unheard of, mostly because it is so difficult to accomplish. After Hurricane Katrina, a group of Benedictine monks in southern Louisiana began selling low-cost, handmade cypress caskets. The state's Board of Embalmers and Funeral Directors drummed up a cease-and-desist order, claiming that only funeral homes licensed by their board could sell "funeral merchandise." Eventually a federal judge sided with the monks, saying it was clear there was no public health risk from the sale of the caskets, and the motivation of the board was solely economic protectionism.

Legally and logistically, circumventing the funeral industry and its regulations to create a nonprofit death service for a community is nearly impossible. In this landscape, where funeral boards are coming after monks — monks! — it is a challenge to convey how truly astounding the accomplishments at Crestone are.

The morning after the funeral in Crestone, I entered the cremation circle and was greeted by two adorable dogs bounding around the pyre. McGregor, Stephanie's brother and volunteer ash gatherer, had arrived early that morning to sift through Laura's remains, four and a half gallons of bone and cinders. From the ash pile he pulled out the largest bone fragments — chunks of femur, rib, and skull — which some families like to take home and keep as relics.

There were significantly more ashes in this pile than after a typical commercial cremation, which leaves only as much remains as can fit in a Folgers coffee can. In California, we are required to grind the bones in a silver machine called a Cremulator until they are "unrecognizable bone fragments." The state frowns on distributing the larger, recognizable bones to the family.

Several of Laura's friends wanted a portion of the ashes, and any excess would be scattered in the hills around the pyre or further into the mountains. "She would have loved that," Jason said. "She's every-

where now."

I asked Jason if anything had changed for him since the cremation yesterday. "My mom brought me up to see the pyre the last time I visited. I was confused, I thought that I was going to have to sit on that bench there and cremate my mom alone, all by myself. It seemed so morbid. Three days ago I was horrified at what I was coming to Crestone to do. But Mom had told me, 'This is what I've chosen for my body, you can come or not.' "

When Jason arrived for his mother's wake in her home, things began to shift. By the time of the cremation, he had realized that he had a whole community by his side. There were talks and songs, and he allowed himself to be supported by everyone who loved his mother. "That was moving to me. It changed things."

Crouched down over the ashes, McGregor explained to Laura's son Jason what they were looking at. He demonstrated how brittle the bones were after being subjected to the heat, crumbling a small fragment into ash with his hand.

"What's this?" Jason asked, pulling out a small piece of metal from the pile. It was the iridescent face of a Swatch watch that Laura had been wearing when she was brought to the pyre. Warped into rainbow colors by the heat of the fire, it was stopped forever at 7:16 a.m. — the moment the flames took hold.

INDONESIA:
SOUTH SULAWESI

There is a remote region in Indonesia where people are present with their dead at a length we can't even begin to conceive — the holy grail of corpse interaction. For years I thought visiting this place was beyond my reach. But I had forgotten one crucial thing: I knew Dr. Paul Koudounaris.

One day in the spring, I sat in the home of Dr. Paul, scholar of the macabre and longtime Los Angeles cult treasure. By sat, I mean I perched directly on the hardwood floor. Paul's home in Los Angeles, which he calls the "Moroccan pirate castle," has no furniture. There are, however, clusters of taxidermied animals, Renaissance paintings, and Middle Eastern lanterns suspended from the ceiling.

"I'm going to Tana Toraja for the *ma'nene'* in August," he said, with a nonchalance only Paul can pull off. For the last twelve years he has traveled all over the world photographing everything from burial caves in Rwanda, to Czech churches decorated in human bone, to mummified monks in Thailand covered head to toe in gold leaf. This is a guy who, in order to transport himself to rural Bolivia, caught a ride on a World War II paratrooper plane that hauled frozen meat. The only other passengers were a farmer, his pig, his sheep, and his dog. When the plane hit turbulence, the animals scattered. As Paul and the farmer lunged to capture them, the copilot turned and screamed, "Stop shaking the plane, you're going to make us crash!' " Paul is the type of person who can handle a trip to Toraja.

Then, he invited me to tag along. "But to warn you, the trip itself is a pain the ass."

Several months later we touched down in Jakarta, the largest city in Indonesia. Indonesia is made up of more than 17,000 islands and boasts the fourth largest population in the world (behind China, India, and the United States).

To catch our next flight we shuffled through passport control.

"Where are you traveling to in Indonesia?" asked the pleasant young woman at the desk.

"Tana Toraja."

An impish grin crossed her face. "You are going to see the dead bodies?"

"Yes."

"Oh — really?" She seemed taken aback, as if her initial question was just to make polite conversation. "The dead bodies, do you know, are they walking by themselves?"

"No, the family holds them up. They aren't like zombies," Paul replied.

"I'm afraid of them!" She turned to share a nervous laugh with her coworker in the next booth as she stamped us through.

When we finally arrived in Makassar, the capital of the island of South Sulawesi, I had been awake for thirty-nine hours. As we exited the airport into the heavy air, Paul was swarmed like a celebrity. I forgot to mention that Paul in person looks just as outlandish as his house — a claim I lay with the utmost aesthetic respect. He has thick dreadlocks, a beaded wizard's beard, and tattoos. He traveled in a purple velvet frock coat and a top hat with an ermine skull attached to the brim. No one knows his age. He was once described by a mutual friend of ours as "an eighteenth-century highwayman reimagined by Tim Burton." Paul refers to himself as "a cross between Prince and Vlad the Impaler."

Men ceased their frantic taxi hawking in

order to get a closer look at Paul's tattoos and his skull hat. Paul's visual strangeness gets him through locked doors and into secret monasteries and bone caves that no one else would have access to. People are too confounded to refuse him.

There was no time for a nap at a hotel. We found our driver and were whisked away on our eight-hour drive north. Green rice fields stretched out on either side of the road and water buffalo plopped languidly into baths of mud.

As we navigated the southern lowlands, we heard the Muslim call to prayer pumped through the speakers of roadside mosques. The majority of Indonesians are Muslim, but in the remote mountains of Tana Toraja, the people followed an animistic religion called Aluk to Dolo ("the way of the ancestors") until the Dutch introduced Christianity in the early 1900s.

We hit the mountains not long after. Our driver barreled the SUV up winding two-lane roads, dodging and swerving around mopeds and trucks in a never-ending game of automobile chicken. Not speaking his language, I finally had to act out the universal symbol for "Seriously, bro, I'm going to vomit."

By the time we arrived in Toraja, I was

starting to hallucinate from lack of sleep. But Paul, who had enjoyed multiple naps on the plane, wanted to photograph a series of nearby burial caves before dark.

There was no one at the Londa burial caves when we pulled up. Up against the cliff, set on rickety scaffolding, were stacks of coffins made of uru wood, shaped like boats, buffalos, and pigs. Radiocarbon dating shows that coffins like these have been used in Toraja since 800 BC. Skulls peeked out of cracks in the wood like nosy neighbors, watching our arrival. As the wood of the coffins decomposes, the bones they contain will go rolling and spilling down the side of the cliff.

Even more surreal, the coffins sat next to rows and rows of *tau tau,* the Torajans' realistic wooden effigies of the dead, seated like an important village council. They represent the souls of the anonymous bones scattered in the cave. The older *tau tau* are crudely carved, with oversized white eyes and straggled wigs. More modern *tau tau* are distressing in their realism, with finely lined faces, convincing warts, and veined skin. They wear eyeglasses, clothes, and jewelry, and look ready to pry themselves up by their canes and welcome us in.

Inside the darkened cave, skulls lined the

crevices and natural ledges in the stone. Some were artfully arranged in pyramid-shaped stacks and rows, while some were left upside down. Some were bleached white, and others were vivid green, covered in moss. Some had cigarettes posed jauntily in their mouths. A lower jawbone (missing the rest of its skull) smoked two cigarettes at once.

Paul motioned me to follow him through a small hole, to what I imagined was another chamber of the cave. Crouching and squinting into the darkness, I saw that this move would require crawling on my stomach through a tunnel.

"Yeah, that's okay, I'll stay here."

Paul, who sometimes breaks into aban-

doned copper and pumice mines in the Los Angeles area (because, of course he does), crawled away. The tails of his velvet frock coat disappeared into the hole.

My cellphone, my only source of light, was at 2 percent battery life, so I powered it down and sat in the dark among the skulls. Minutes went by, maybe five, maybe twenty, when a lantern broke through the darkness. It was a family: a mother and several teenagers, Indonesian tourists from Jakarta. From their perspective, I must have looked like a possum trapped by car headlights against a garage wall.

In gracious, elevated English, a young man positioned himself at my elbow and said, "Excuse me, miss. If you will direct your at-

tention to the camera, we will create an Instagram."

Flashes started going off, sending my image to #LondaCaves. Strange as this felt in the moment, I could see why the discovery of a six-foot-tall white girl in a polka-dot dress in the corner of a cave filled with skulls would be an Instagrammable moment. They took several pictures with me in different poses before moving on.

I woke refreshed after fourteen comatose hours in our hotel in the city of Rantepao. We went to meet our guide, Agus — pronounced "Ah Goose" — in the lobby. He was compact and fit, handsome. Agus had been taking Dutch and German tourists on deep jungle and rafting treks for twenty-five years, but in recent years had developed a special death-focused relationship with Paul. Agus told us that the *ma'nene'* (the ritual we had come to see) wouldn't happen until tomorrow ("on Toraja time"). Today's adventure would be an appetizer to the *ma'nene':* a Torajan funeral.

We wound down endless dirt roads in Agus's SUV, through the emerald green hills. For several miles we were caught behind a moped with a hairy black pig tied down with neon green rope behind the

driver. I scooted forward in my seat. Was the pig dead? As if on cue, the pig's hooves went into swimming motion.

Agus caught me looking. "Pigs are harder to carry on a bike than a person. They squirm."

The pig was heading to the same Torajan funeral we were. One of us would not be coming back.

You could hear the funeral before you saw it: drums and cymbals crashing. We entered the swirl of people following behind the corpse. The body was being transferred in a replica of a traditional Torajan house. These houses, known as *tongkonan,* resemble no residence you've ever seen, standing high on stilts with a roof that swoops up to two points in the sky. This corpse, inside his mini-house, was carried atop the shoulders of thirty-five young men.

The crowd jostled into a central courtyard as the corpse made its way around the periphery. It was slow going — the house was heavier than expected and the men had to stop every thirty seconds or so and set it down.

In the center of the courtyard stood a buffalo, robust and serious in its demeanor. The buffalo's presence implied a vague threat of what was to come. Staked to the ground by a short rope, it looked like the lamb left out for the hungry T-Rex in *Jurassic Park.* As Chekhov said about the theater, if you reveal a gun on stage in Act I, it better go off by the final act.

Tourists (at least, the ones I could tell were tourists because of their white skin and Western European accents) were corralled in the far back corner of the courtyard. This is the primary tension of Toraja's death tourism industry: how to get tourists close, but not too close. Our exile in Section J seemed more than fair to me, and I plunked myself down to observe as Paul set up his camera for photographs. Today he wore an outfit better suited to the humid weather:

denim overalls, a sheriff's badge, polka-dot socks, and a cowboy hat.

There were some tourists who did not get the hint. One couple perched themselves in folding chairs alongside the dead man's family in the VIP section. The locals were too polite to ask them to leave. An older German woman with crudely dyed blond hair walked directly into the center of the courtyard, through the unfolding festivities, taking photographs with her iPad thrust into local children's faces and chain-smoking Marlboro Reds. I wanted to yank her out with a vaudeville cane.

Tourism in Tana Toraja is a recent development, almost unheard of before the 1970s. The Indonesian government had concentrated on developing tourism (to great success) on other islands like Bali and Java, but Tana Toraja had something those other places didn't: impressive, ritualistic death. They no longer wanted to be viewed by the rest of Indonesia as a place of "headhunters and black magic," but as participants in a high culture tradition.

The corpse made its way into the courtyard. The men carrying the house thrust it up and down, chanting and grunting. They went at it until they exhausted themselves and had to set the whole house down, then took a deep breath and did it again. It was hypnotic to watch the surging effort, especially compared to the staid pace of a standard pallbearers' procession in the West.

The corpse was (*is,* if you're Torajan) that of a man named Rovinus Lintin. He was important to the village, a government worker and farmer. Behind me stood a five-foot-high color poster of Rovinus's face. The image showed a man in his late sixties in a sharp blue suit and a pencil-thin John Waters mustache.

Children in elaborate beaded costumes ran through the courtyard, dodging the men carrying squealing pigs tied to bamboo stakes. The men were taking the pigs to a hidden back area. The door of the main house was closed off by a hanging tapestry featuring a full roster of Disney princesses; Belle, Ariel, and Aurora watched the pigs pass to the slaughter. I wondered if moped-pig from earlier in the day was among them.

These Torajan funerals are not casual B.Y.O.B(uffalo) events. Each pig and sacrificial animal had been brought by a different family, and carefully recorded. There is a system of debts that keeps people coming to funerals for years. As Agus said, "You bring a pig to my mother's funeral now, I will bring one for you someday." Torajan

and American death culture share this particular trait of overexpenditure; no one wants to be perceived as disrespecting the dead.

All of these rituals might seem complicated, but Agus claimed they have actually become far less so. His parents were born into the animistic Aluk religion, but his father converted to Catholicism at age sixteen. Agus gave his theory: "There are 7,777 rituals in Aluk. People left because it got too complicated." Catholicism hardly seems the place to go for fewer complicated rituals, but there you go.

The crowd went silent as the priest came over the loudspeaker and began his sermon. I didn't understand the words, but he punctuated his speech with salutes to the deceased, booming "RO-vinus LIN-TOOOOOOON!" at top volume. For twenty minutes he spoke, and when he started to lose the crowd with the repetitive phrasing he screamed into the microphone, like a death metal rocker, "COOOOO-EEEEE!" Let me tell you, if you're sitting next to a speaker and don't see a "COOOOOEEEEE!" coming, it can be devastating. Agus translated the expression as something akin to "listen up!" In recent years the narration at Torajan funerals (as well as choreography and costume choices) has taken cues from television variety shows.

Rovinus had died — as Western medicine would define the term — at the end of May, three months earlier. But according to Torajan tradition, Rovinus remained living. He might have stopped breathing, but his physical state was more like a high fever, an illness. This illness would last until the first animal, a buffalo or a pig, was sacrificed. After the sacrifice, *ma'karu'dusan* ("to exhale the last breath"), Rovinus could at last die alongside the animal.

During his two years of fieldwork in Toraja, anthropologist Dimitri Tsintjilonis developed a close friendship with a local woman named Ne' Layuk, who referred to Dimitri as one of her children. He came back to Toraja nine years later, excited to surprise Ne' Layuk with his joyous return, only to discover she had died two weeks prior to his arrival. Dimitri went to visit her corpse and was led into the back room by a family member, who announced to Ne' Layuk that Dimitri was "back."

Looking at her face, I crouched down by her side and whispered my greetings. Although one side of her face seemed to be slightly crumbling, she looked serene

75

and composed . . . she was only "asleep" (mamma') and she "knew" (natandai) I was there. More than that, she could hear and see me; in fact, she was not "dead" (mate); she was only ill ("hot") and "could feel everything" (nasa'dingan apa-apa).

In Toraja, during the period of time between death and the funeral, the body is kept in the home. That might not sound particularly shocking, until I tell you that period can last from several months to several years. During that time, the family cares for and mummifies the body, bringing the corpse food, changing its clothes, and speaking to the body.

The first time Paul ever visited Toraja, he asked Agus if it was unusual for a family to keep a dead relative in the home. Agus laughed at the question. "When I was a child, we had my grandfather in the home for seven years. My brother and I, we slept with him in the same bed. In the morning we put his clothes on and stood him against the wall. At night he came back to bed."

Paul describes death in Toraja, as he's witnessed it, not as a "hard border," an impenetrable wall between the living and the dead, but a border that can be transgressed. According to their animistic belief system, there is also no barrier between the human and nonhuman aspects of the natural world: animals, mountains, and even the dead. Speaking to your grandfather's corpse is a way to build a connection to the person's spirit.

The priest had gone silent, his last "COOOOOEEEEE!" fading mercifully from the loudspeaker. Paul sidled up beside me and whispered, "After they sacrifice the buffalo, maybe one of the tourists should be next."

As if on cue, two men walked toward the buffalo. One threaded a blue rope through its metal nostril ring. The man was gentle with the buffalo, scratching its chin. The buffalo seemed not to notice it had become the center of attention. The second man squatted down to tie the buffalo's front hooves to wooden stakes in the ground.

I was expecting — I'm not sure — another chant, a gathering of family members? But it took only seconds for the man to lift the buffalo's chin by the rope, pull a machete from his belt, and slice directly into its throat. The buffalo reared back into the air, its powerful muscles and horns on display. It attempted to flee, but the rope kept it in place. There was a vivid red gash on its throat, but no blood was falling. The first cut was not deep enough.

Several more men rushed forward, grabbing at the rope strung through the buffalo's nose, but the buffalo wasn't having it. It bucked and thrashed, exposing its severed windpipe to the crowd. It was not easy to watch. The man pulled out a machete from his belt, giving the neck a second chop. This time the buffalo's throat pulsed electric red blood.

The buffalo jerked back with enough force to break itself free from the wooden stake. It stumbled to the right and barreled into the crowd. There was chaos, screaming. The footage from my small video camera went into *Cloverfield* mode, heavy breathing and sweeping shots of the ground. The crowd surged around me and I sliced my hand on the edge of a concrete pillar.

I was sure someone (probably me) would

fall victim to the buffalo's revenge, but the celebrants caught it and dragged it back to the center, where at last it fell still, its blood pouring into a pool of red foam around its throat. The crowd's keening noises and nervous laughter bloomed into a complex polyphony. The danger had brought the funeral to life.

Agus was on a heated phone call.

"What's the deal?" I asked Paul.

"We need to bring a pig."

"Where are we going to get a pig?"

"Agus is finding one. It's rude to show up without a pig."

The SUV was already full. There was me, Paul, Agus, the driver, and Atto, a fifteen-year-old boy catching a ride to the distant village. There was no room for a pig.

Agus hung up the phone and announced, "Tomorrow my friend will bring the pig on his moped."

Atto was texting furiously the whole ride, as you would expect from a teenager trapped in a car with adults. During the *ma'nene'*, the graves of his uncle and his great-grandfather would be opened. Both men had died before Atto was born, so he'd only ever met them as corpses.

The village had no central square, but was

a series of isolated hamlets. The majority of its people were rice farmers, including our hosts. They lived in seven *tongkonan* (the sweeping Torajan homes on stilts) situated around a communal courtyard. Plump roosters crowed. Skinny dogs chased the roosters and laughing children chased the dogs. Women were beating the recently harvested rice with tall bamboo poles in a mesmerizing, repetitive motion.

People trickled in to the village to begin cleaning the ten or so house-graves that stood in a cluster. Heavy padlocks on the grave doors were a new development; it's not that the neighbors didn't trust one another, but a few years prior a mummy had been stolen from the village and taken to Rantepao for sale to a collector. The villagers were tipped off as to who had taken it, and went to Rantepao to steal it back.

A group of men gathered to discuss the logistics of house-grave ventilation. A villager named John Hans Tappi had been placed in one of the graves two years earlier. You could see his dark wood coffin propped up in the corner, through the open door. Tappi's son feared the air inside had been too wet, too humid. "I hope my father is still okay, still mummified, and has not gone rotten."

This would be an important *ma'nene'* for John Hans Tappi. His son felt that when John died two years before, his family had not been able to do enough for him financially. They could not afford to sacrifice a buffalo in his honor and the slight had haunted the son ever since. He believed that by not slaughtering the buffalo, "my father was not carried to the second life." That would change this week; the buffalo was already selected and waiting in a nearby field.

Two house-graves over, a woman pulled open the door and sprayed an industrial-sized can of lemon air freshener inside.

Up the road a family had slaughtered a pig and were awaiting the arrival of a Protestant priest to bless their new grave, which would hold six family members. They asked if we wanted to join them for dinner.

Chunks of the pig's flesh were cubed and placed in bamboo tubes to be cooked over the fire. The pig had been butchered right next to the fire where it now roasted. Pools of pig blood stagnated as we ate, and several lazy flies buzzed around us. The severed hooves hung from a nearby bamboo scaffolding. A small dog dashed in and made off with a piece of the pig's offal, still dripping blood and fluid. "Ey!" the fire-tender yelled after the beast, but left the dog alone to enjoy his prize.

A woman offered me a bamboo leaf with a pile of warm pink rice on top. The bamboo tubes were pulled hot from the fire, the flesh still sizzling. Many of the pig chunks were pure fat. Halfway through the meal I held up the bamboo leaf and looked closer at the crisp, fatty skin and saw the hair follicles, still visible. This is the flesh of a dead animal, I realized, and was for the moment repulsed.

For as much time as I had spent facing human mortality, I didn't recognize a dead animal that didn't come wrapped in plastic and Styrofoam. French anthropologist Noëlie Vialles wrote of the food system in France, though this could be said of almost any country in the West: "slaughtering was required to be industrial, that is to say large-scale and anonymous; it must be non-violent (ideally: painless); and it must be invisible (ideally: non-existent). It must be as if it were not."

It must be as if it were not.

An old woman, so old her eyes had clouded over with cataracts, picked at a small pile of rice and gazed out over the valley. She didn't interact with anyone around her; maybe she no longer could.

Agus poked me with a pork-stained finger and whispered, "This grave will be hers." He was making fun of her, but also speaking a basic fact. This woman would soon go the way of her ancestors, and would move into this new yellow house, "the house without fire and smoke."

Later that night, our pig arrived on the moped. It promptly took up residence under one of the houses and chomped away on food scraps, unaware that Paul and I had brought it here to meet its demise.*

That night we slept in the belly of the *tongkonan* house. It seemed enormous from the outside, so we were surprised to climb up the wooden ladder and discover a single, windowless room. Bedding was laid out on the floor, and we fell into a grateful sleep. It was only later in the night that we realized we were wrong about the lone room. Wooden latches in the wall opened into three other rooms. All night long people quietly crawled in and out of the walls around us.

* When we did the math, I owed Paul $666 for the pig, the hotel, and Agus's services as a guide. My 2015 tax return had a write-off for a $666 sacrificial pig.

■ ■ ■ ■

The next morning began with the sound of a plaintive gong tolling along the village road. This announced the official start of the *ma'nene'*.

The first mummy I saw wore eighties' style aviator sunglasses with yellow-tinted frames.

"Damn," I thought, "that guy looks like my middle school algebra teacher."

One young man stood the mummy up as another sliced into its navy blazer with a pair of scissors, cutting all the way down to his pants, revealing the torso and legs. Given that this gentleman had been dead eight years, he was remarkably well preserved, with no obvious gashes or breaks in his flesh. Two coffins down, another fellow hadn't been so lucky. His body was now entirely shriveled, nothing left but thin strips of dried skin over bone, held together by gold embroidered cloth.

Wearing nothing but boxer shorts and the aviators, the mummy was placed on the ground, a pillow beneath his head. An eight-by-ten-inch framed portrait photo, taken during his life, sat propped next to his body. Alive, he had looked far less like my math teacher than he did today, eight years into mummification.

A group of women fell to their knees beside the man and keened, wailing his name and stroking his cheeks. When their wails softened, the man's son moved in with a set of paintbrushes — the kind you'd buy at the local hardware store. The son began to clean the corpse, brushing his father's leathery skin with short, loving strokes. A cockroach scampered out from inside the boxer shorts. The son didn't seem to mind, and carried on brushing. This was mourning as I had never seen it before.

Ten minutes earlier, Agus had received a call that there were mummies being unwrapped at a hard-to-reach grave by the river. We sped in that direction, running along a narrow dirt path through a rice field. The path ended in a ditch of brown water. With no ford or bridge, we groaned and plowed through the thick mud. I slid down an embankment on my butt.

When we arrived at the site, almost forty bodies had been removed from their house-grave and lined up in rows on the ground. Some were wrapped in brightly colored cloths, some were in slender wooden coffins, and some were wrapped in cartoon quilts and blankets — we're talking Hello

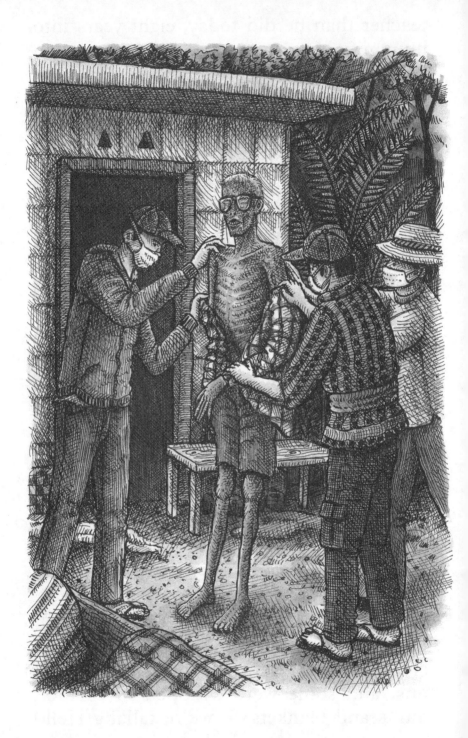

Kitty, SpongeBob Squarepants, and various Disney characters. The family moved from body to body, deciding whom to unwrap. Some were unknown; nobody remembered exactly who they were. And some were top priority — a beloved husband or daughter whom they missed and couldn't wait to see again.

A mother unwrapped her son, who had died when he was only sixteen. At first, all that could be seen was a crooked pair of feet. Hands emerged, and seemed well enough preserved. Men on either side of the coffin pulled gently on the body, testing to see if they could lift it without the body crumbling. They managed to stand him vertical, and though his torso had been preserved, his face was skeletal, excepting his teeth and thick brown hair. His mother didn't seem to mind. She was ecstatic to see her child, even for a moment, even in this state, and held his hand and touched his face.

Nearby a son brushed the skin of his father, whose face was stained pink from his batik wrapping. "He was a good man," he said. "He had eight children but he never beat us. I'm sad, but happy, because I can care for him as he did for me."

The Torajans talked directly to the

corpses, narrating their next move: "Now I am removing you from the grave," "I brought you cigarettes, I'm sorry I do not have more money," "Your daughter and family have arrived from Makassar," "Now I remove your coat."

At the grave by the river, the leader of the family thanked us for coming, and for bringing several boxes of cigarettes. He welcomed Paul to take pictures and me to ask questions. In return, he requested, "If you see any other outsiders to the village, do not tell them about this place, it is secret."

I flashed back to the boorish German woman at the funeral, cigarette hanging from her mouth, iPad shoved in people's faces. I feared I had become that woman. Our desire to see something we had anticipated for months had driven us where we weren't wanted.

We went back through the rice field, returning to the main road, to find that our host family had at last begun to remove and unwrap their dead. I recognized a man my age who worked as a graphic designer in Rantepao. He had arrived on his moped late the night before, climbing out of the wall as I slept. He pulled out a skeleton wrapped in gold fabric. "This is my brother, he died in a motorbike crash when he was seventeen." He pointed to the wrapped body next to him. "That is my grandfather."

Down the hill from us, another family had laid out a picnic, complete with a gingham blanket, for their grandfather, who had died seven years earlier. This was his second appearance at a *ma'nene'* ceremony and he was still in good shape, preservation-wise. His family brushed his face with a grass broom and flipped him over, peeling dried flesh from the back of his head. They stood him up for a family portrait, and the family gathered round, some stoic, some smiling. I was observing off to the side when a woman called me over to join the picture. I waved my hands, as if to say, "Nope, terrible idea," but they insisted. Somewhere deep in Indonesia, there exists a picture of me with a Torajan family and a freshly cleaned mummy.

I had heard of mummification occurring in very dry or very cold climates, but the lush, humid air of Indonesia hardly fell into that category. So how did the dead of this village become mummies? The answer depended on who you asked. Some claimed they would only mummify the body in the old way — pouring oils into the person's

mouth and throat, and spreading special tea leaves and tree barks on the skin. The tannins in the tea and bark bind with and shrink the proteins in the skin, making it stronger, stiffer, and more resistant to bacterial attack. The process is similar to how a taxidermist would preserve an animal hide (hence the word "tanning" in leather).

The new trend in Torajan body mummification is none other than good ol' embalmer's formalin (a solution of formaldehyde, methyl alcohol, and water) injected into the body. One woman I spoke to did not want her family members to receive the more invasive injections, but said in a conspiratorial tone, "I know other people are doing it."

The villagers in this region of Toraja are amateur taxidermists of the human body. Given that the Torajans now use similar chemical formulas as North Americans to mummify their dead, I wondered why Westerners are so horrified at the practice. Perhaps it is not the extreme preservation that offends. Rather, it is that a Torajan body doesn't sequester itself in a sealed casket, walled in a cement fortress underneath the earth, but instead dares to hang around among the living.*

Confronted with the idea of keeping Mom in the house for seven years after her death, many Westerners picture the movie *Psycho* and its deranged hotel manager. The Torajan villagers preserve the corpses of their mothers; Norman Bates preserved the corpse of his mother. The villagers live with their bodies for many years; Norman lived with his mother's body for many years. The villagers have conversations with their bodies as if they are alive; Norman had

---

*Which raises the question, why preserve the body so intensely if you're *not* planning to keep it around, America?

conversations with his mother's body as if she were alive. But while these villagers spend an afternoon cleaning the graves, exuding a mundane normalcy, Norman Bates is the American Film Institute's second scariest movie villain of all time, coming in behind Hannibal Lecter and ahead of Darth Vader. He didn't win that sinister acclaim by murdering innocent hotel guests wearing his mother's clothing; he won it because Westerners feel there is something profoundly creepy about interacting with the dead over a long period of time. (I've spoiled *Psycho* entirely — apologies.)

Yesterday I had met the son of John Hans Tappi. Today I was going to meet John Hans himself. He was laid out, basking in the sun in plaid boxer shorts and a gold watch. His chest and abdominal cavity had been infused with formalin when he died, which explained why two years later his torso was flawlessly preserved, while his face had gone black and pockmarked, revealing bone below. When the family had to clean inside his boxers and brush around his mummified penis, they looked just as uncomfortable as you would expect. They made a self-deprecating joke and got the job done.

Small children ran from mummy to

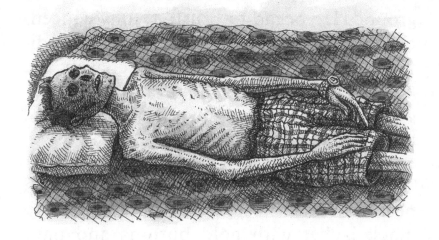

mummy, inspecting and poking them before scampering away. One girl, about five years old, climbed up the side of a house-grave to join me on the edge of a roof, above the bustle below. The two of us sat in silence, bound by a kinship of awkwardness, of preferring to watch from above.

Agus spotted me up there and yelled, "Look, makes me think about how I'm going to be like this. This is going to be me, eh?"

Back at the house where we were staying, a four-year-old boy watched us eat bowls of rice. He popped his head up from behind a railing and squealed with delight when I made faces back. His mother told him to leave us alone, so he found a paintbrush. He moved through the courtyard and squatted next to a dried bamboo leaf on the ground. He began to brush it, fully concentrated, hitting all the crevices. If the tradition of the *ma'nene'* continues, chances are he will grow up to do that to a body, perhaps one of the people that we met here in the village.

The next morning John Hans Tappi had been redressed in new clothes, a button-up black jacket with gold buttons and navy slacks. He was making a move today, to a new house-grave down the road, light blue and topped with a white cross. The decoration on the grave was a cultural mix: traditional symbols of the buffalo, but also the sacred heart of the Virgin Mary, photos of Jesus praying, and a full rendering of the Last Supper.

John Hans's family propped him up and posed with him for one final picture in his new garb before placing him back in his coffin. They put his shiny black dress shoes next to his feet, and pulled blankets over him, tucking him in. Closing the lid, they polished the sides, and carried the coffin down the road on their shoulders, drumming and chanting as they went. That was the end of the excitement for John Hans, until three years later when he would emerge again.

As I loaded the SUV, Agus remarked, "You know there is a body in that house?" He pointed to the Torajan house next door to the one we had been sleeping in, all of ten feet away. The family had been waiting to see how we'd react before telling us about a woman called Sanda, a seventy-year-old who had died two weeks earlier.

"Do you want to see her?" Agus asked.

I gave a slow nod: somehow, it made perfect sense that we had been snoozing corpse-adjacent our entire stay.

"Hey, Paul," I whispered up the ladder up to our sleeping quarters. "I think you want to get down here."

On Agus's instructions, we brought the remainder of our food to offer to Sanda — she would know we had brought it. We climbed into the back room, where Sanda lay on a dried bamboo mat. She was under a green plaid blanket, wearing an orange blouse and a pink scarf. Her purse was next to her, with food laid out. Her face was wrapped in cloths and had the rubbery texture I had seen so often in embalmed bodies.

Sanda had been preserved with formalin, injected by a local specialist. The family couldn't do the injections themselves be-

cause the chemical formula was "too spicy" for their eyes. As successful rice farmers, Sanda's family did not have the time to tend to her body each day, as the old ways would require.

Until she goes to her house-grave she will live with her family. They bring her food, tea, and offerings. She visits them in their dreams. It had only been two weeks since she passed through the soft, porous border with death. After the odor had dispersed, her family planned to sleep in the room with her.

Agus — who, remember, slept with his dead grandfather for seven years as a child — shrugged. "For us, we are used to it, this kind of thing. This life and death."

Before arriving in Indonesia, I struggled to find descriptions of what rituals I would see in this area of Tana Toraja. Recent accounts — at least in English — are scarce. (Googling the *ma'nene'* directs you to NeNe Leakes, the Real Housewife of Atlanta.)

Pictures are rare as well: the best images I could find appeared in the British tabloid the *Daily Mail.* I don't know where they got the pictures; they certainly didn't send a correspondent. The online comment section fascinated me. "OMG, whatever happened to RIP?" said one commenter. "Seriously, this is sooooooo disrespectful," added another.

And indeed, had the commenter disinterred Aunt Sally from the local cemetery in Minnesota and driven her corpse around a suburban neighborhood in a golf cart, yes, that would be disrespectful. The commenter hadn't grown up believing that familial relationships continue after the death of the body. For Torajans, hauling someone out of their grave years after their death is not only respectful (the *most* respectful thing they can do, in fact), but it provides a meaningful way to stay connected to their dead.

Being a mortician means everyone asks me questions about their mother's dead body. You have no idea how often I hear: "My mother died eleven years ago in upstate New York, she was embalmed and buried in the family plot, could you describe what she'd look like now?" The answer depends on too many factors: the weather, the soil, the casket, the chemicals; I can never give a good answer. But as I watched the Torajan families interact with their mummified mothers, I realized that they don't need to inquire with a mortician about the state of their mother's body. They know perfectly well what Mom is up to, even eleven years after her death. Seeing Mom again, even in this altered state, might be less frightening than the specters of the human imagination.

MEXICO: MICHOACÁN

A skeleton, wearing a black bowler hat and smoking a cigar, swooped down Avenida Juárez, his long bony arms waving madly. At fifteen feet tall, he towered above the teeming crowds. Trailing behind him, men and women cavorted and danced dressed as Calavera Catrina, the iconic dapper skeleton. A cloud of glitter shot out of a cannon as a phalanx of Aztec warriors twirled by on rollerblades. The crowd, tens of thousands strong, cheered and chanted.

If you have seen the 2016 James Bond film *Spectre,* you will recognize this spectacle of flowers, skeletons, devils, and floats as Mexico City's annual *Días de los Muertos,* or Days of the Dead, parade. In the opening scene of the film, Bond glides through the mêlée in a skeleton mask and tux and slips into a hotel with a masked woman.

Except, here's the trick. The *Días de los Muertos* parade did not inspire the James

Bond film. *The James Bond film inspired the parade.* The Mexican government, afraid that people around the world would see the film and expect that the parade exists when it did not, recruited 1,200 volunteers and spent a year re-creating the four-hour pageant.

To some, the parade was a crass commercialization of the very private, family-centered festival that is *Días de los Muertos* — the two days at the beginning of November when the dead are said to return to indulge in the pleasures of the living. To others, it was *Días de los Muertos*'s natural progression to a more secular, nationalistic holiday, boldly celebrating Mexico's history in front of a worldwide audience.

When the parade was over, we trudged

through the sparkle carnage left by the glitter cannons. My companion was Sarah Chavez, the director of my nonprofit The Order of the Good Death. She pointed out the *Días de los Muertos* decorations that hung everywhere, in homes and businesses: *calaveras* and bright paper cutout skeletons.

"Oh!" She had remembered something important. "I forgot to tell you, they sell *pan de muerto* at the Starbucks by our hotel!" *Pan de muerto,* or bread of the dead, is a roll baked with raised human bone formations and topped with sugar.

The next day we would be traveling west to Michoacán, a more rural area where families have long celebrated *Días de los Muertos*. But here in Mexico City, there was a period in the early twentieth century when

101

Días de los Muertos fell out of popular favor. By the 1950s, Mexicans in urban areas viewed celebrating the Days of the Dead as outmoded folklore, practiced by people at the outskirts of civilized society.

In an intriguing twist, one of the main motivators in changing that perception was the southward creep of Halloween from the United States. In the early 1970s, writers and intellectuals came to view Halloween as, in the words of journalist María Luisa Mendoza, a *"fiesta gringa"* with "witches on a broom and pointy hats, cats, and pumpkins that are a pleasure to read about in detective books but are absolutely unconnected to us." Mendoza wrote that her fellow Mexicans were ignoring the children who begged for pennies and cleaned car windshields just to survive, while in rich neighborhoods, "our bourgeoisie mimic the Texans and allow their children to go into others' houses dressed ridiculously and to ask for alms, which they *will* receive."

During this time, as scholar Claudio Lomnitz wrote, the Days of the Dead "became a generalized marker of national identity" that stood "opposite of the Americanized celebration of Halloween." Those who had once rejected the *Días de los Muertos* (or who lived in areas where it had never been practiced at all) came to see the celebration as very Mexican. Not only did *Días de los Muertos* return to major cities — looking at you, James Bond parade; the festival also came to represent the struggles of many disenfranchised political groups. These groups adopted *Días de los Muertos* to mourn for those kept from the public eye, including sex workers, indigenous and gay rights groups, and Mexicans who had died trying to cross the border to the U.S. In the last forty years, *Días de los Muertos* has come to represent popular culture, tourist culture, and protest culture throughout Mexico. And Mexico itself is viewed as a world leader in practicing engaged, public grief.

"I grew up with elders that were self-hating Mexicans," Sarah explained, as we sat in our hotel room in Michoacán the next day. "They were taught they had nothing to be proud of and everything to be ashamed of. They needed to assimilate. To be happy in America was to be as white as possible."

Sarah's grandparents moved from Monterrey, Mexico, in the early twentieth century and settled in the East Los Angeles neighborhood known as Chavez Ravine. In 1950, the government sent letters to the

1,800 families of Chavez Ravine, mostly low income Mexican American farmers, informing them that they would have to sell their homes to make way for public housing. The displaced families were promised new schools and playgrounds and housing priority when the developments were finished. Instead, after removing the families and destroying a community, the city of Los Angeles scrapped the public housing plan and partnered with a New York businessman to build Dodger Stadium. Supporters of the new stadium, including Ronald Reagan, called the critics "baseball haters."

Mexican Americans from Chavez Ravine were driven further east of Los Angeles by discriminatory housing practices. Sarah's parents came of age in this environment of displacement. They had Sarah when they were both nineteen.

"To this day, when my grandmother and aunts and uncles talk about Chavez Ravine, they are heartbroken. They miss it so, so much," Sarah said.

When Sarah was born, she was not allowed to learn Spanish. She had lighter skin, which made her the favorite grandchild. Her Mexicanness was confined to the home. Growing up in Los Angeles, she bounced between a distant mother, her Hollywood costumer father (who to this day identifies not as Mexican, but as 'American Indian'), and her grandparents. Sarah grew comfortable being an American who happened to be Mexican, but felt little tangible connection to her family's culture.

In 2013, after ten years as a preschool and kindergarten teacher, Sarah fell in love with her partner Ruben⋆ and the pair felt ready for a child of their own. She became pregnant. To Sarah, this child represented a chance "to be a *real* family, *my* family, a *chosen* family, something no one could take away from me."

This dream was not to be. Her son died when she was six months pregnant. The months that followed the death were a time of "nobody and nothing." Sarah was estranged from her parents. She felt alone. There were days when she wanted to wander into the field of orange trees behind her house and disappear. Then there was the blame: Did I lift a heavy thing the wrong way? Did I eat the wrong thing? "The archetypal woman is as a bringer of life," Sarah said, "but my body was a tomb."

Sarah felt radioactive to all her friends and coworkers. She knew people wanted to live

⋆ His name has been changed.

in a world where children are precious and invulnerable. "I was asked by society to hide my grief," she said. "They didn't want to confront such horrors. I was the face of those horrors. I was the boogeyman."

Sarah scoured the Internet for stories from other mothers who had suffered the death of a child. She found websites made by well-meaning women, often with a very Christian overtone (e.g., "my angel has taken his place in the Lord's arms") and stories that offered platitudes and euphemisms. To Sarah, these feel-good pick-me-ups were nothing but empty clichés. The accounts could not capture the wrenching agony and longing that she felt.

Searching for comfort, she landed on the doorstep of her own heritage. "Sarah, you're Mexican. You come from arguably one of the most death-engaged cultures in the world," she thought. "How would your ancestors deal with this tragedy?"

Mexican poet Octavio Paz famously said that while citizens of Western cities like New York, Paris, and London would "burn their lips" if they so much as uttered the word "death," "the Mexican, on the other hand, frequents it, mocks it, caresses it, sleeps with it, entertains it; it is one of his favorite playthings and his most enduring love."

This is not to say Mexicans have never feared death. Their relationship with death was hard-won; it emerged after centuries of brutality. "Rather than becoming a proud and powerful empire," Claudio Lomnitz explained, "Mexico was bullied, invaded, occupied, mutilated, and extorted by foreign powers and independent operators alike." In the twentieth century, as the Western world reached its peak of repression and death denial, in Mexico a "gay familiarity with death became a cornerstone of national identity."

For Sarah, coming to terms with her son's death wasn't an attempt to erase her fear of mortality; she knew such a task was impossible. She just wanted to engage with death, to be allowed to speak its name. As Paz said: frequent it, mock it, caress it.

Many children and grandchildren of immigrants, have, like Sarah, found themselves severed from their family's cultural rituals. The funeral system in the United States is notorious for passing laws and regulations interfering with diverse death practices and enforcing assimilation toward Americanized norms.

In a particularly heartbreaking example, many Muslims would like to be able to open funeral homes in the U.S. and serve their communities as licensed funeral directors. Islamic custom is to wash and purify the body immediately after death before burying it as quickly as possible, ideally before nightfall. The Muslim community rejects embalming, recoiling at the idea of cutting into the body and injecting it with chemicals and preservatives. Yet many states have draconian regulations requiring funeral homes to offer embalming and all funeral directors to be trained as embalmers, despite the fact that the embalming process itself is never required. Muslim funeral directors must compromise their beliefs if they want a chance to help their community in death.

Sarah's first, and most lasting, gateway into Mexican culture was the work of the painter Frida Kahlo, Mexico's *heroína del dolor,* the heroine of pain. In her 1932 painting *Self-Portrait on the Borderline between Mexico and the United States,* a defiant Frida straddles an imaginary boundary between Mexico and Detroit, where she was living at the time with her husband, the muralist Diego Rivera. The Mexican side is strewn with skulls, ruins, plants, and flowers with thick roots burrowed deep into the soil. The Detroit side contains factories, skyscrapers, and plumes of smoke — an industrial city that hides the natural cycle of life and death.

While living in Detroit, Kahlo became pregnant. She wrote of the pregnancy to her former physician, Leo Eloesser, her devoted correspondent from 1932 to 1951. She worried that pregnancy was too dangerous, that her body had been damaged by the famous streetcar accident that shattered part of her pelvis and punctured her uterus. Kahlo reported that her doctor in Detroit "gave me quinine and very strong castor oil for purge." When the chemicals failed to end the pregnancy, her doctor declined to perform a surgical abortion, and Kahlo faced the prospect of carrying the risky pregnancy to term. She begged Eloesser to write to her doctor in Detroit, "since performing an abortion is against the law, maybe he is scared or something, and later it would be impossible to undergo such an operation." We don't know how Eloesser responded to Kahlo's request, but two months later, she suffered a violent miscarriage.

In a painting she created after her experience, *Henry Ford Hospital (La cama volando),* Frida lies naked on a hospital bed, the sheets soaked with blood. Objects float in the space around her, attached to her stomach by umbilical cords made of red ribbon: a male fetus (her son), medical objects, and symbols like a snail and an orchid. Detroit's stark, manufacturing skyline disturbs the background. Regardless of her visceral distaste for Detroit and the horrible misfortune that occurred there, art historian Victor Zamudio Taylor claims it was here that "Kahlo, for the first time, consciously decides that she will paint about herself, and that she will paint the most private and painful aspects of herself."

For Sarah, adrift amid a sea of "God has a plan for you" banalities, the frankness of Kahlo's art and letters served as a balm. In Kahlo she saw another Mexican woman forced to grapple with impossible choices for her child and her own body. Kahlo was able to project this pain and confusion through her work, portraying her body and her grief without shame.

Sarah's son died in July 2013. In November of that same year, she and her partner Ruben, who is also Mexican American, visited Mexico during *Días de los Muertos*. "We weren't coming to 'visit' death. We weren't tourists," Sarah said. "We were living with death every single day."

Among the elaborate altars for the dead

110

and the very public images of skulls and skeletons, Sarah found both the confrontation and the peace that she hadn't found in California. "Being in Mexico, it felt like a place to lay down my grief. It was recognized. I wasn't making other people uncomfortable. I could breathe."

Among the places they visited was Guanajuato, home to a famed collection of mummies. In the late nineteenth century, bodies buried in the local cemetery were subject to a fee, a grave tax, for "perpetual" interment. If the family couldn't pay the fee, the bones were eventually removed to make room for a fresh body. During one such disinterment, the city was shocked to

discover that they were not digging up bones but "flesh mummified in grotesque forms and facial expressions." The soil's chemical components, along with the atmosphere in Guanajuato, had naturally mummified the bodies.

The city continued to unearth mummified bodies over the course of six decades, cremating the less impressive mummies and putting the truly expressive ones on display in the town museum, El Museo de las Momias.

Author Ray Bradbury visited these mummies in the late 1970s and wrote a story about them, adding that "the experience so wounded and terrified me, I could hardly wait to flee Mexico. I had nightmares about dying and having to remain in the halls of the dead with those propped and wired bodies."

Because the mummies were not intentionally preserved by the hands of other humans but naturally mummified by their environment, many of them have gaping mouths and twisted arms and necks. After death, the body reverts to "primary flaccidity" — all of the muscles in the body relax, dropping the jaw open, loosening tension in the eyelids, and affording the joints extreme flexibility. In death, corpses don't hold

themselves together. They no longer have to play by the living's rules. The visual ghastliness of the Guanajuato mummies was not designed to "terrify" Mr. Bradbury, but a result of the bodies' normal postmortem bioprocesses.

The mummies, still on display, did not have the same confronting effect on Sarah. She turned a dark corner and stopped in front of the mummified body of a small baby girl, dressed in white and lying on velvet. "She looked like an angel with this halo of light around her, and I swear that in that moment I felt like I could stand there forever and just look at her."

Another woman noticed Sarah's silent

tears and went to get her a tissue, quietly holding her arm.

Other child mummies in the museum had their own props, such as scepters and crowns. These were the *Angelitos,* or Little Angels. Prior to the mid-twentieth century in Mexico and elsewhere in Latin America, a dead baby or child was considered a spiritual being, almost a saint, with a direct audience with God. These *Angelitos,* free from sin, could offer favors for the family members they left behind.

The godmother would prepare the body, washing and dressing it in the garb of a pint-sized saint, and surround it with candles and flowers. The mother wouldn't see the corpse until after this process, at which point the body had relinquished the burdens of grief, transformed into a heavenly being ready to take its place by God's right side.

Friends and family were invited to the party, not only to honor the child but also to impress and gain its favor; remember, it now possessed great spiritual power. Sometimes the child was even carried from party to party, with other children acting as the pallbearers, with the parents and family in procession. Often the *Angelito* was photographed or painted amid a brilliant tableau.

For Sarah, though she holds no belief in the saints or the afterlife, it was the recognition of the child's death that moved her. "These children were treated as so special. Something was done just for them," she said. There were parties and paintings and games and, most of all, tasks to perform for the child — tasks beyond the lonely, interminable silences.

Each year, on the evening of November 1, the border between the living and the dead thins and frays, allowing the spirits to transgress. Out on the cobblestone streets of Santa Fe de la Laguna, a small city in Michoacán, old women bustled from house to house carrying *pan de muerto* and fresh fruit, visiting their neighbors who had lost someone that year.

I ducked my head under an entryway draped in golden marigolds. Right above the door hung a framed picture of Jorge, who was only twenty-six years old when he died. In the photo he wore a backwards baseball cap. Behind him were posters from bands. "Slipknot? I don't know about that, Jorge," I thought, wondering if it was bad form to judge the dead for their taste in music. "Oh, the Misfits! That's a good choice."

Through the entryway was Jorge's three-tiered altar, or *ofrenda*. Each item his family and friends brought to his altar was designed to entice him home that night. Since Jorge died that year, his family erected his altar at the family home. In years to come they will move the offerings to Jorge's grave at the cemetery. He will continue to return as long as his family continues to show up, inviting him to come back among the living.

At the base of his altar was a black chalice of copal incense, its pungent aroma wafting into the air. Candles and marigolds adorned a three-foot-tall pile of fruits and breads. The pile would only grow as the evening went on and more members of the community stopped by to make their offerings. When Jorge returned he wouldn't be a corpse reanimated, but a spirit, consuming the bananas and breads on his own spiritual plane.

At the center of his altar was Jorge's favorite white T-shirt, illustrated with a sad clown and "Joker" written in script. A bottle of Pepsi awaited his return (the appeal of which I understood — gross as it sounds, I'd come back from the dead for a Diet Coke). Further up there was more traditional Christian imagery, several Virgin Marys and a very bloody crucified Jesus. Strung from the ceiling were colorful paper cutouts of skeletons riding bikes.

About a dozen members of Jorge's family gathered around the *ofrenda,* preparing to receive visitors until late into the night. Toddlers ran underfoot wearing sparkly princess dresses, their faces painted as skeletal *catrinas.* They held small pumpkins for gathering candy from adults.

Sarah had come ready with a bag full of candies. Word got out among the children, and she was swarmed with *catrina*-faced kids with their pumpkins, many with lit candles inside. *"Señorita! Señorita, gracias!"* Sarah dropped down to their level, doling out the candy with the calm, loving disposition of the elementary school teacher she had once been. "We made these same pumpkins with candles in them for *Días de los Muertos* in my classroom every year, but one little fire and the administration makes you stop," she said with a wry smile.

Santa Fe de la Laguna is home to the Purépecha, an indigenous people known for their unique pyramid architecture and their feather mosaics made from prized hummingbirds. In 1525, with a population debilitated by smallpox, and aware that the formidable Aztecs had already fallen to the Spanish, their leader pledged allegiance to Spain. Today, school in the region is taught bilingually, in both Purépecha and Spanish.

Many of the elements that welcome the dead today — the music, the incense, the flowers, the food — were already in use among the indigenous people before the Spanish conquest in the sixteenth century. At the time of the *conquista,* a Dominican friar wrote that the native people were happy to adopt the Catholic festivals of All Saints and All Souls because they provided the perfect fronts for their existing festivals honoring the dead.

Attempts were made over the ensuing centuries to eradicate the practices, which were "above all, horrifying to the illustrious elite, who sought to expel death from social life." In 1766, the Royal Office of Crime banned the indigenous population from gathering in their family cemeteries, cruelly cutting them off from their dead. But the customs, as they so often do, found a way to persist.

Over one home in Santa Fe de la Laguna, a sign in Purépecha read, "Welcome home, Father Cornelio." Cornelio's altar took up an entire room. I laid my bananas and oranges atop a growing pile, while the family's matriarchs swooped in to offer us large, steaming bowls of *pozole* and mugs of *atole,* a hot drink of corn, cinnamon, and chocolate. For the families, this night is not just a one-way acceptance of offerings for their dead; it is an exchange with the community.

Observing the action from the corner of the room was Father Cornelio himself, in the form of a full-sized effigy. Effigy Cornelio sat on a folding chair, wearing a poncho, black high-tops, and a white cowboy hat tilted down, as if taking an afternoon snooze.

In the center of the altar was a framed photo of Cornelio in which he wore the same white cowboy hat as his effigy. A wooden cross rose up behind the picture. Hanging from the cross were the iconic *calaveras,* or brightly colored sugar skulls . . . and bagels. "Sarah, is it normal to hang

119

bagels off the altar?" I asked.

"Yes," she said. "You'll see a lot of bagels."

After visiting several family homes to make offerings, I asked Sarah which altar had most moved her. "The happiest time was not with the altars, it was with the children." She gestured to a boy, three or four years old, toddling past with his pumpkin bucket, wearing a Superman cape. "It's bittersweet. Right now, my son, he would be exactly that age." Bashful, the little Superman held out his bucket for candy.

We continued our journey south to the larger town of Tzintzuntzan, which holds a raucous street festival during *Días de los Muertos.* Vendors cook pork and beef on large metal skillets, music blasts from speakers outside local businesses, children pop firecrackers in the streets. Up a gently sloping hill, at the edge of town, sits the local cemetery.

Walking into the cemetery on the evening of November 1 was nothing short of revelatory. The cemetery glowed with the light of tens of thousands of candles, which the families plan and save all year to provide for their returning dead. A small boy worked diligently at his grandmother's grave, relighting or replacing any of the hundreds of

candles that had been snuffed out. The
candles' radiance mixed with the smell of
marigolds and incense, creating a golden
haze drifting among the graves.

In recent years, many cities in the United
States have begun holding events for *Días
de los Muertos,* including a massive celebration at Hollywood Forever Cemetery. Hollywood Forever is only minutes down the
road from my funeral home in L.A., and I
have attended the celebration several times.
Hollywood's celebration is impressive in
scale and execution, but in feeling and emotion it falls miles short of Tzintzuntzan's. It
felt safe inside the walls of this cemetery,

like being in the center of a glowing, beating heart.

Baskets sat atop the cement platforms of the graves, so the dead who returned would have something to carry their offerings back in. Small wood fires burned, keeping the gathered families warm. A band, made up of trombones, trumpets, drums, and a massive tuba, moved from grave to grave, playing songs that sounded, to my untrained ear, like *ranchera* mashups of mariachi and college fight songs.

Sarah stopped at the grave of Marco Antonio Barriga, who died at only one year old. A picture of Marco showed a dove flying above him. His grave was a fortress, seven feet high, reflecting the size of his parents' grief. Marco had died twenty years before, but his grave was still covered in candles and flowers, proof that the pain of losing a child never goes away.

Before coming to Mexico, I had known that Sarah's son had died. But I did not know the circumstances. Alone in our hotel room, she revealed the devastating truth.

At Sarah's first ultrasound, a chatty technician slid the wand over Sarah's stomach and suddenly fell silent. "I'm going to bring the doctor in," she announced.

At the second ultrasound, the specialist

was astonishingly blunt. "Ah, I see a club foot here," she narrated, "this hand has three fingers; this hand has four. Poor development in the heart. Oh, look — he has two eyes, though! Most don't." And then the final kick to the gut: "I just don't think this pregnancy is going to be viable."

Sarah's baby had trisomy 13, a rare chromosomal condition that causes intellectual and physical abnormalities. Most babies born with the condition will not live beyond a few days.

A third doctor told Sarah, "If you were my wife, I would tell you not to carry this pregnancy to term."

A fourth doctor offered two grim choices. The first was to induce labor in the hospital. Her baby would live outside the womb a very short time, and then die. The second was to terminate the pregnancy. "I know someone in Los Angeles who can do this for you," the doctor said. "She doesn't usually perform the procedure this late, but I'll call her for you."

At this point, Sarah was almost six months pregnant. She made the appointment. She tried to distance herself from her baby to prepare for what was coming, but he was kicking inside her. She didn't want him taken away. "He wasn't something foreign inside me; he was my son."

To end a pregnancy at such a late stage required three appointments over three days. A line of protestors blocked Sarah and Ruben's path to enter the clinic. "One particularly vile woman screamed over and over that I was a murderer. I couldn't take it, so I walked directly up to her and screamed in her face, 'My baby is already dead! How dare you!' "

They waited in the clinic for an hour, listening to the faint screams of the protesters outside: "Hey, lady with the dead baby! Listen, we can still save you!"

These were the three worst days of Sarah and Ruben's lives. A final ultrasound was required. Sarah turned away from the monitor, but Ruben saw their baby moving its hand, as if waving goodbye.

In another room Sarah could hear the wrenching sobs of a young girl who had tried to end her life because she was pregnant. "I don't want it! I don't want it!" the girl screamed.

"I wanted to comfort her, and tell her I would take her baby," Sarah thought, "but that wasn't really what I wanted. I wanted *this* baby, my baby."

On the last day of the procedure, the whole staff came in and stood around her operating table and told Sarah how very sorry they were this had happened, and how they promised to take good care of her. "This is where people treated me with the most kindness," Sarah said, "in the place that was, for me, a place of death."

More than three years later, the weight of her son's death is like a constant anchor in Sarah's body. In the cemetery in Tzintzuntzan, as Sarah stared at the photo of baby Marco, Ruben lovingly rubbed the small of her back. She broke the silence. "Parents just want to show off their baby. They are so proud. If their baby dies, that opportunity is taken away. This is their chance, to show they still love their child, they are still proud of him."

Instead of pride, Sarah felt the opposite when her son died. She felt pressure to maintain her "dignity" and to keep her grief silent, lest her visceral trauma depress anyone else.

The Western funeral home loves the word "dignity." The largest American funeral corporation has even trademarked the word. What dignity translates to, more often than not, is silence, a forced poise, a rigid formality. Wakes last exactly two hours. Processions lead to the cemetery. The family leaves the cemetery before the casket is even lowered into the ground.

In the cemetery we found grave after grave memorializing young children, including Adriel Teras de la Cruz. He was born on what would have been Sarah's due date, and lived just over a week. His parents sat at his graveside. A small girl lay on her mother's chest, and an older boy was tucked up under a blanket next to the grave, sound asleep.

Adopting or adapting the customs of the *Días de los Muertos,* argues Claudio Lomnitz, could end up saving the emotional lives of Mexico's neighbors to the north. He writes that Mexicans "have powers of healing, and of healing what is certainly the United States' most painfully chronic ailment: its denial of death . . . and its abandonment of the bereaved to a kind of solitary confinement."

On our last day in Mexico, we returned to Mexico City, and we visited the home of Frida Kahlo, the famous Casa Azul. It was in this house that Kahlo was born, and where she died at age forty-seven. "As outlandish and weird as this sounds, coming here is almost an act of gratitude," Sarah explained. "Frida helped me. La Casa Azul is a pilgrimage."

"I think most mothers have at least some fear of being imprisoned by the birth of a child," Sarah said. "I'm always aware of all the things I can do, all the places I can travel, these pilgrimages I can take, because I don't have a young child. I'm aware of all the time I have. It makes it more valuable, because I possess this time at a terrible cost."

On display in La Casa Azul was Kahlo's painting *Frida and the Cesarean,* an unfinished work that depicts Frida with a split stomach, lying next to a full-term baby. Sarah gasped when she saw it. "This is my first in-person meeting with one of these pieces. It's like making friends with a person online and then meeting them face to face, in real life. It's emotional."

Frida Kahlo's true feelings on bearing children may never be entirely clear. Some biographers are so keen to protect her saintly image that they have rebranded her medical abortions as the devastating "miscarriages" of an otherwise eager mother. Other biographers insist that Kahlo was uninterested in children and that her "poor health" was just an excuse to duck the cultural expectation of raising a family.

Upstairs, in Kahlo's small bedroom, there was a pre-Columbian urn containing her ashes. On her single bed lay Frida's death mask, an eerie reminder that the artist had bled and died in this very room. Above her bed Frida had hung a painting: a dead infant, swaddled in white, wearing a flower crown, lying on a satin pillow: an *Angelito*.

NORTH CAROLINA: CULLOWHEE

The grey whale is an impressive creature — fifty feet long and weighing over thirty-six tons, with formidable flukes spanning ten feet. A dozen miles off the coast of California, she emerges into view and exhales with a final, weakened puff. After sixty-five years, death has come for the great beast, and she hangs limp at the surface.

Some whales begin to sink straightaway, but this particular whale will remain afloat. Inside the carcass, tissues and proteins are breaking down, organs are liquefying, and gases are building up — they are filling the whale's blubbery outer casing, transforming her into a macabre balloon. If she were to be punctured in a single spot, the force of the pressurized gases would launch her mushy innards several yards from her body. But this whale's skin holds. Gases slip out slowly; our former cetacean deflates and begins her gradual descent to the sea floor below. Down, down she goes, traveling more than a mile, until at last the beast meets soft bottom.

Down here in the bathyal (or midnight) zone of the ocean, it is cold and completely dark — sunlight does not reach these depths. Our whale hasn't come down here to "rest in peace" and lie on the ocean floor in cool, undisturbed darkness. Her remains are about to become the location of a grand banquet that will last decades. This process, known in the ocean science community as a whale fall, creates an entire ecosystem around the carcass — like a pop-up restaurant for the alienlike creatures of the primordial depths.

The mobile scavengers smell the whale and arrive first to feast. They are the quintessential otherworldly denizens of the deep: sleeper sharks, hagfish (an unfair name — they're more like slime-producing eels than fish), crabs, and ratfish. They begin tearing into the decomposed flesh, consuming up to 130 pounds a day.

Once the bulk of the organic material has been picked clean, the area around the carcass becomes a hotspot of life on an otherwise barren seabed. Mollusks and crustaceans set up camp. A thick red fuzz of deep-sea worms grows on the whale's bones,

45,000 of them per square meter. The worms' Latin name, *Osedax,* means "bone devourer." True to that designation, these eyeless, mouthless creatures will burrow into the bones and extract oils and fats from within them. Recently, scientists have discovered that the sulfur-loving bacteria present at a whale fall are similar to those found in deep-sea hydrothermal vents.

The site of the whale fall turns into a decades-long version of "Be Our Guest" from *Beauty and the Beast,* a debauched, celebratory party where creatures devour the whale "course by course, one by one." The whale is the epitome of a postmortem benefactor, part of an arrangement as beautiful as it is sensible — an animal dying and donating its body so that others may thrive. "Try the grey stuff, it's delicious," the carcass seems to say. The whale, in short, is a valuable necrocitizen.

To be fair, science has yet to determine how whales *feel* about this state of affairs. Given the chance, would they prefer to forgo the whale fall and have their carcasses locked up in an impenetrable coral reef fortress somewhere? A postmortem safe haven, perhaps, but one that would prevent other animals from benefiting from the vital nutrients that are no longer of use to the departed whale?

Whales spend their whole lives supporting the environment that surrounds them. Their diet is fish and krill, and for years humans assumed that *fewer* whales = *more* fish and krill for us. This equation justified the whaling industry's slaughter of almost three million whales in the twentieth century alone.

As it turns out, fewer whales does not mean more fish. Whales dive down to the shadowy depths of the ocean to feed. They must return to the surface to breathe, and while there, they release robust fecal plumes. (Note: Poop, they're pooping.) The whale poop is full of iron and nitrogen, which trickle down to fertilize plankton, which — you guessed it — fish and krill depend upon to live and thrive. Whales are a crucial part of this cycle during their lives, and in death they are no different.

Instinctually, you may feel the same pull to contribute past your own death. How else to explain the increasing popularity of the refrain: "When I die, no fuss. Just dig a hole and put me in it."

A sensible request, indeed. Sending your corpse back into nature would seem to be both the most inexpensive and the most "green" option for your death. After all, the plants and animals we consume during our lives are grown and nourished by the soil.

A single acre of soil can contain 2,400 pounds of fungi, 1,500 pounds of bacteria, 900 pounds of earthworms, 890 pounds of arthropods and algae, and 133 pounds of protozoa. The soil teems with life, as does the dead body (inside its sausage casing of keratin, or dead skin). Microscopic sorcery takes place when a body is placed just a few feet deep in the soil. Here, the trillions of bacteria living inside you will liquefy your innards. When the built-up pressure breaks the seal of skin an orgiastic reunion takes place, in which our bodies merge with the earth.

We owe our very lives to the soil, and, as William Bryant Logan said, "the bodies we give it back are not payment enough." Though, presumably, they are a start.

"How would you describe what we're doing here, Katrina?"

She thought for a moment before replying, "We're setting up the experiments."

"What are the experiments?"

"Wait, let's not call them 'experiments,' that makes it sound like I'm a mad scientist."

"What's a better word than experiments?"

"We're here setting up *the mounds.* No,

that's equally creepy. Dammit."

I waited.

"Let's just say we're tweaking the mound recipe," she decided, only half satisfied.

You have to be careful with language if you're Katrina Spade, the person leading the charge, as the *New York Times* put it, to "turn corpses into compost." It is a delicate sales pitch, a proposal that toes the line between eco-death innovation and the deranged Soylent Green scheme of a charlatan.

Katrina and I drove up the winding roads of southern Appalachia, the Blue Ridge Mountains that straddle the border between Tennessee and North Carolina. Here, as in the rest of the United States, the modern funeral industry has seeped in and taken over the rituals and logistics of deathcare. But because of the isolation, religion, and poverty of the area, the creep of industrialized death took longer here than almost anywhere else in the country.

At last, we turned down an isolated road and pulled up at a gate. Dr. Cheryl Johnston — Dr. J, as her students called her — was already there, joined by a small group of undergraduate volunteers. Dr. J runs the Forensic Osteology Research Station (FOREST) at Western Carolina University.

You might have heard this type of facility described as a "body farm," where corpses, donated to science, are laid out to decompose for forensic study and law enforcement training. But, as Dr. J is quick to point out, "body farm" is an inaccurate term: "A farm grows food. We don't *grow* bodies. Considering our end product, you could call it a skeleton farm, I guess?"

I was giving the side-eye to some silver tarps covering what looked to be dirt burial mounds. "Do they place the donor bodies under there? Right where we park the cars?" I wondered. I had seen many a dead person in my day, but they were all nonthreatening, lying on sterile white tables and gurneys. It makes you uneasy when a body is somewhere it's not "supposed" to be, like seeing your chemistry teacher at the supermarket.

"Nope," Dr. J said, after introductions were made. "They're not human. Those are the black bears. Roadkill. Sometimes the Department of Natural Resources brings us fifteen to twenty a year. Their fur is so black that they're pretty easy to hit with your car at night."

The bear burials (*bearials,* if you will) acted as practice for the undergraduates. After a bear decays down to bone, the

137

students set up a systematic grid and collect the bones to bring back to the lab for examination. Successfully processing a bear permits a student to work on the human beings, located not in the parking area (I was pleased to discover) but in a 58-by-58-foot pen up the hill, fenced in with razor wire to keep out the curious, which include coyotes, bears, and drunk college students.

The group trudged up the hill to the pen's padlocked gate, which Dr. Johnston opened. Stepping inside, I wasn't hit by a pungent smell or an eerie sense of death. Instead, this tiny pen for corpses in the North Carolina mountains was picturesque as hell, with dappled sunshine pushing through the trees and hitting the voluptuous under-growth. At present it held the remains of the fifteen souls that had come to rest in the facility postmortem — three bodies buried beneath the soil, twelve exposed on top.

The bones of a female skeleton in purple polka-dot pajamas had scattered due to runoff from the spring rainstorms. Her skull had come to rest down near her femur. Several yards to her left a man, more recently dead, had a jaw that yawned open, hanging by a thin layer of flesh that held his mandible in place. If you knelt next to him you could see the amber facial hair poking through.

Katrina gestured up the hill to a splayed skeleton. "When I was here a few months ago that guy still had a mustache and the most beautiful marbled blue skin. He didn't smell so great, though." Then, seeing as he was lying right there, she apologized. "Sorry, it's true."

The idea to compost the dead first came to Katrina when she was working on her master's degree in architecture. While other students aped the work of Rem Koolhaas and Frank Gehry, Katrina was designing a "resting place for the urban dead." She saw her future clients as the deceased denizens of the modern metropolis, comfortable with a life in the concrete jungle, but longing in death to return to the natural world, where "flesh becomes soil."

Why attempt to compost, though, when

the obvious way to address the primeval yearning to have "flesh become soil" would be to open more natural or conservation burial cemeteries, where corpses could go straight into a hole in the ground — no embalming, no caskets, no heavy concrete vaults? Katrina responds, correctly, that overcrowded cities are unlikely to assign huge swaths of valuable, developable land to the dead. And so she aims to reform not the market for burial, but for cremation.

The result of Katrina's thesis was the Urban Death Project, an architectural blueprint for body composting centers in urban areas. The centers would be scalable worldwide, from Beijing to Amsterdam. Mourners would carry the dead person up a ramp built around a central core made of smooth, warm concrete, two and half stories tall. At the top, the body would be laid into a carbon-rich mixture that would, in four to six weeks' time, reduce the body (bones and all) to soil.

The compost reaction occurs when you mix things that are high in nitrogen (think food waste, grass clippings, or . . . a dead human body) into a pile of material high in carbon (think woodchips or sawdust). Adding a dash of moisture and oxygen causes the microbes and bacteria inside the pile to begin breaking down the organic tissues and releasing heat. This gets the whole thing cooking. Temperatures inside the compost pile often reach 150 degrees, hot enough to kill most pathogens. With the right balance between carbon and nitrogen, the molecules will bind, creating incredibly rich soil.

"During those four to six weeks you're in the core, you'd cease to be human," Katrina explained. "Molecules literally turn into other molecules. You transform." This transformation of molecules is what inspired the name she's given the process: recomposition ("corpse composting" being about three degrees too intense for the general public). At the end of the recomposition, the family can collect the soil to place in their garden, and a mother who loved to garden can, herself, give rise to new life.

Katrina was 99 percent confident we could recompose a human, and she had an impressive roster of soil scientists on her advisory board who thought that her confidence should be at 100 percent. After all, they had been composting livestock for years. The chemical and biological processes that break down a 1,000-pound steer should work just as well on a measly 180-pound human. But she needed experimental evidence on real live (well, real dead) human remains.

This is where Dr. Johnston and the FOREST facility came in. Dr. J was intrigued by Katrina's idea for studying human composting, but hadn't planned immediate experiments. Then, serendipitously, she inherited a small mountain of woodchips from the on-campus recycling program. Shortly after, she got a call that a new donor body was on its way to the facility. So she texted Katrina: "I've got a body. Should we try?"

In February 2015, that first donor body, a seventy-eight-year-old female (we'll call her June Compost) was laid in a bed of pure woodchips at the bottom of the hill at FOREST. A month later, the body of a second donor, a larger male (we'll call him John Compost) was placed at the top of the hill in a mix of alfalfa and woodchips with a silver tarp pulled over the mound. The experiments were not overly sophisticated. The sole question that these two donor bodies were answering was, "Will they compost?"

At FOREST today there was a brand-new donor body to worry about, set to arrive at the facility in an hour. His name was Frank, a man in his sixties felled by a heart attack earlier in the week. Before his death, Frank chose to donate his body to the human decomposition facility.

"Does Frank's family know about the whole composting thing?" I asked Dr. Johnston.

"I talked to the brother, Bobby, several times," Dr. J explained. "I made it clear, 'You can say no to this, and Frank will be used for regular forensic study.' But the family insisted this is what Frank would have wanted. To be honest, by the time you sign up to donate your body to a place like this, you're up for pretty much anything."

To prepare for Frank's arrival, we had begun shoveling and hauling a giant pile of pine and maple woodchips up the hill in five-gallon painter's buckets. The physical exertion didn't faze Katrina, who was tall and lean with a short pixie haircut. Even in her late thirties she reminded me of the popular soccer player from high school, and practically bounded up the hill with the buckets.

One of the undergraduates, a blond, strapping young man, could haul four buckets at a time, two in each hand.

"You are a student here?" I asked.

"Yes ma'am, I am. A senior in forensic anthropology," he drawled. For self-preservation I attributed the "ma'am" as a Southern thing, rather than a sign of my advancing age.

Hauling woodchips in the North Carolina sun (at which I made a valiant effort, I would like to add) seemed like manual labor, and didn't give me the same sense of deathcare Zen as raking the ashes out after a cremation.

By 11 a.m. we had created a two-foot base layer of woodchips at the top of the hill in the pen. It only lacked a willing victim, our man Frank. As if on cue, a navy blue van rolled into the parking area. Two men entered the facility wearing pressed khakis and matching blue polo shirts with Crowe Funeral Home logos. They were a father and son funeral team, the elder Crowe with white hair, the younger Crowe with blond.

The Crowes had never been to the FOREST facility, so Dr. Johnston began by giving them a tour. I could see their faces scrunch in confusion, calculating exactly how they were going to get the donor body Frank up multiple embankments and through the undergrowth. The elder Crowe broke the news to Dr. J: "He's a bit of a bigger fella."

People die in inconvenient places all the time (armchairs, bathtubs, backyard sheds, the tops of high perilous staircases). But funeral directors usually remove bodies *from* these places, not deposit them *into* these places. Funeral work prides itself on taking a dead body from chaos to order, not the other way around.

I asked the elder Crowe if this was one of the strangest removals he'd done in a while.

He looked over his shoulder, and with a dry tone, rewarded me with a "Yeah." Full stop.

Calculations were made for a route that provided solid footing without disturbing the other residents of the FOREST facility. On their messy journey to skeletonization, the donor bodies are disturbed by rainwater and small creatures. At FOREST, it was all too easy to accidentally tromp on someone's rogue fibia if you didn't take precautions.

The elder and younger Crowes pulled a stretcher up to the entrance gate, with Frank's electric blue hospital body bag riding on top. The vibrant blue color stood in stark contrast to the muted greens and browns of the North Carolina summer. The toe tag attached to the bag read "Western Carolina University — Urban Death Project." Katrina flipped the tag to take a look. Her mouth tugged up in the smallest smile. She later told me she felt a jolt of legitimacy to see that name in print.

Father Crowe chatted with Dr. Johnston.

To my surprise, his inquiries weren't along the lines of "Tell me again what y'all crazy-quacks are trying to do out here?" but had already moved to "So, are you using alfalfa to release nitrogen faster?" Father Crowe was a composter himself, and was well versed in the technicalities of the process. In a corporatized funeral industry, where I've heard a natural burial described as a "hippie myth that *our* clients would never want," it was a joy to see a more traditional funeral director present himself as an unexpected ally to a somewhat radical idea.

Unfortunately for Katrina, winning over

the funeral industry won't be her only challenge. Mike Adams, a popular blogger (also an anti-vaxxer, 9/11 truther, and Sandy Hook shooting skeptic), wrote about Katrina in an article shared almost 11,000 times on Facebook. Adams viewed the recomposition project as being solely geared toward growing food for the urban populace. Since the new world order would need a steady supply of human compost to keep people fed, it would surely lead to "the forced euthanasia of the elderly so that their bodies can be tossed into the composter." Adams claimed that the project would be "used by the government to greenwash mass murder."

Knowing Katrina, a Seattle-based ecoenthusiast with a partner and two children, the idea of her masterminding mass murder seems preposterous. But the public relations issue remains: for every person who believes it is destiny for their body to nourish the earth, there is a person who thinks Katrina's plan represents society at its most debauched and depraved.

Soon enough the struggle to get Frank up the hill began. It was a team effort, starting with a lengthy feet-first vs. head-first debate. At one point I looked over and saw a skull gazing down from its perch at the top of the hill, observing the absurdity of us living folk below.

When Frank finally arrived at the top of the hill (head-first), the blue body bag was laid on the bed of woodchips and unzipped, revealing a tall, sturdy man, naked except for underwear and socks. We rolled Frank over on his right side and gently wiggled the bag free, so it was man on woodchip, no turning back.

Frank had a white goatee and shoulder-length hair, and his left arm was draped almost elegantly behind his head, "draw me like one of your French girls" style. Tattoos covered his torso and arms: a wizard, serpents, religious symbols, a T-Rex galloping across his chest. The ink added bursts of color to the forest floor.

The undergraduates retreated down the hill to gather more alfalfa mixture, and I was left alone with Katrina for the first time all morning.

She gazed down at Frank, her eyes wet around the edges. "This man, he's here on purpose. You know? He *wanted* to be here."

She paused, took a breath before continuing, "I am filled with gratitude."

Katrina took a handful of green alfalfa and wood chips, and placed the mixture over Frank's face, the first part of his body to be covered.

I joined in, and the two of us blanketed the mixture down his neck and around his arms, almost tucking him in. "We're making a little nest for him! It looks comfy," Katrina said.

She stopped, scolding herself. "Dr. J wouldn't want us to be this sentimental with the bodies. Cut it out, Katrina."

I wasn't so sure. Earlier in the day Dr. Johnston had told me a story about a man in his eighties who donated his body to FOREST. After he died, his wife and daughter drove his body to the facility in the family truck. They were even allowed to pick a spot in the underbrush for him. Then, only six months later, his wife died. She requested that her body be laid out in an area next to her husband. That request was honored, and man and wife decayed into the earth side by side, together as they had been in life. So much for no one being sentimental.

Dr. J was unapologetic in this attitude. "I like to call the donors 'Mr. So-and-So' or 'Mrs. So-and-So.' Call them by their real names. I don't see a reason not to. It's still them. Other facilities disagree with me and say it is not keeping professional distance. I totally disagree. It humanizes the bodies. I meet some of these people before they die. I know them. They're people."

Dr. J's approach is part of a new wave in scientific donation practices, where a donor body is considered a person, not a nameless cadaver. Ernest Talarico, Jr., is the associate medical director at Indiana University School of Medicine–Northwest. Bodies are donated to his medical school to be dissected by young students in anatomy labs. When Talarico first started with the program, he found himself uncomfortable with the mind-set that the donor bodies were anonymous pieces of flesh, referred to only by numbers or nicknames.

Talarico set up a memorial service, held every year in January, for the program's six donor bodies. In attendance are the first-year medical students and, astonishingly, the families of the donors. Rita Borrelli, who donated the body of her husband to Indiana University, was shocked to get a letter from the students saying they wanted more information on his life. "They even wanted pictures. I was crying so hard I could barely finish reading the letter."

Participation by the family is optional, but allows the students to work through the almost insurmountable task for a modern doctor — honest conversation about death with a family. The students even call their donor body "their first patient." In a profile of the program by the *Wall Street Journal,* first-year medical student Rania Kaoukis explained that "it would have been easier to think of the body as a number. But that isn't what makes good doctors."

With the advent of this enlightened outlook, I asked Dr. J if she would be donating her own body to the FOREST facility when she sloughed off her mortal coil. The answer was yes, in principle. But she was worried about her students. Knowing the donor's personal history and referring to the body as Mrs. So-and-So was one thing. Watching your professor decompose before your very eyes was another. But Dr. J's real barrier was her own mother. Her mother was wholly against the idea of the decomp facility, coming from a generation where a decent funeral meant a wake in a church. She wouldn't donate her body if her mother was alive and uncomfortable with the idea.

Recently, however, Dr. J's mom, musing on what she would like for her own body, announced, "I don't understand why we have to go through this whole cremation or burial rigamarole. Can't we just be brought out to the forest and allowed to decompose naturally?"

"Mom?" Dr. J replied.

"Yes, dear?"

"You know that's what I do, right? That's what the FOREST facility is? A place you decompose in the woods."

Frank's woodchip pile now rose three and half feet. It looked like a Viking burial mound. The strapping blond undergraduate hammered in a wire fence around the mound's lower half to prevent the mulch mixture (or, God forbid, Frank) from escaping and rolling down the hill. This was a far cry from what the recomposition process would end up looking like in an urban setting, but with the birds and cicadas chirping and the speckled sunshine through the trees, I could only think that this would be the perfect place to putrefy.

The volunteer group, covered in sweat and wood dust, reentered the body pen. This time they were hauling water in recycled Tidy Cats litter containers. Twelve gallons were poured over the mound to create moisture to invite microbes and bacteria to the mix. As photos were taken to document the procedure, someone recommended removing the Tidy Cats labels so it wouldn't appear as "Human composting, brought to you by Tidy Cats!" — an association neither side would relish.

Katrina looks to this portion of the process, when the water is poured on top of
the mound, as a future ritual. She doesn't
want the Urban Death Project facilities to
share modern crematories' allergy to family
involvement. She hopes that pouring the
water on fresh woodchips will give the family the same sense of power as lighting the
cremation pyre, pushing the button to start
a modern cremation machine, or shoveling
dirt onto the coffin. As we poured water
onto Frank's mound, it felt like ritual. It felt
like the start of something, for Frank and
perhaps for society.

■ ■ ■ ■

After eating lunch at the town sports bar (we didn't explain to the cheerful blond waiter why we were covered in woodchips), we returned to FOREST. Frank wasn't the only reason we had come to the facility. There was still the matter of June and John Compost, the original donor bodies. Today we would uncover their mounds to see what, if anything, lay beneath.

Trudging back up the hill, Dr. J turned to Katrina and announced, "Oh, I forgot to tell you, the cadaver dogs completely ignored the mounds." Katrina's face lit up.

In her career as a forensic anthropologist, Dr. J had consulted on countless missing person cases, usually centered in the dense woods of the surrounding mountains. After witnessing firsthand the difficulty officials had in locating the dead, Dr. J opened the FOREST facility to law enforcement and search and rescue volunteers with their cadaver dogs. It is a huge benefit to the trainers to have access to real decomposed bodies, in conditions similar to how they might be found in the wild. After a week of training at the FOREST facility, Dr. J sends the trainers home with a sample of what

154

she calls "dirty dirt" — soil from underneath the decomposed bodies, which the officers can continue using for instruction back home. "You should see how thrilled they are when we give them vials of dirt or bits of decomp-soiled clothes. It's like Christmas," Dr. J told me. As the old carol goes, ". . . my true love gave to me, two turtle doves and a dirt vial from under a body."

Why would the cadaver dogs ignoring the composting mounds be a big deal? The dogs work by smell and have no trouble sniffing out bodies laid out in the open, or even those buried in shallow graves. But inside a compost pile, the moisture, aeration, carbon, and nitrogen are balanced to trap the odor within the pile. Katrina is aware that the public will not accept this new method of body disposal if the recomposition facilities, meant to be places of grieving and ritual, reek of human decay. The dogs' complete lack of interest in the body-mounds was great news for the future of the project.

It was decided that the male donor, John Compost, would be uncovered first. He was a tall, burly gentleman in his mid-sixties who had died in March, meaning he had been inside his woodchip and alfalfa pile for five months. His position at the top of the hill meant more direct sunshine, and a higher overall ambient temperature. The whole mound had been covered in a silver tarp.

Digging right into the mound with full-sized metal shovels and spades would run the risk of destroying whatever might be inside. So we used small hand-held shovels and heavy plastic rakes instead. As we cautiously dug into the pile, the bright purple and yellow color of the shovels made us look like children building a morbid sandcastle.

Then, all of a sudden, we hit bone. Dr. Johnston stepped in and used a delicate brush to dust off and reveal the man's left clavicle.

Katrina was crushed by this discovery. "I won't lie. I wanted there to be nothing there. I wanted us to dig and dig and just . . . soil."

Dr. J smiled. "See, I *did* want something to be there."

"Wait," I asked, "we're going for the four-to-six-week complete body compost here, why did you want there to be bones?"

Katrina piped in, "Because Dr. J has different motives, she wants the bones."

Although Dr. J was enthusiastic about Katrina's project, as far as she's concerned there are never enough skeletons. Forensic collections, like the one she runs at Western Carolina, have nowhere near the amount of bones they need. A collection requires a large enough sex and age range to create true, beneficial comparison.

Dr. J believes if she can nail the right removal time from the mounds, she can develop a system that will take a human from flesh to skeleton much faster than the current method — laying them out and waiting for bugs, animals, and nature to do their work.

On the day John Compost was first put in the woodchips, a layer of vivid green alfalfa had been spread over his body in an attempt to raise the temperature of the mound — which it seems to have done. But composting also needs moisture to work, and as we pulled off more of the pile, it became apparent that the alfalfa layer had had the effect of zapping the moisture from his body. John Compost was essentially mummified, his white papery flesh still stuck to the bones along his iliac crest and femur, which I brushed clean in soft strokes. Harsh body composting lesson number one: don't overdo the alfalfa layer.

Dr. J discovered something interesting as she uncovered his head and the top of his right shoulder, the only body parts not covered in the alfalfa. Heavy spring rains had trickled down from the top of the hill and underneath the tarp, soaking that area. Here, far from being mummified, the bones were clean, dark — no flesh to be found. In fact, on his sternum were the beginnings of Swiss cheese-like holes, where even bone had begun to decompose.

Despite that encouraging discovery, John Compost was far from transformed into rich, dark soil, as Katrina had hoped. John had been encased in that mound for five whole months, and there he was, still hanging out, mummified. Livestock composting of a full-grown steer can take as little as four weeks when mechanical aeration is involved. Offal from a butchery only takes five days. Human composting had a long way to go.

Dr. J was unfazed. "You learn a little bit each time," she shrugged, and signaled us to begin covering John up again (after adding more water and dismantling the ill-fated alfalfa layer).

The experiments being done at FOREST recall Italian anatomy professor Lodovico Brunetti's attempts in the late 1800s to create the first modern cremation machine. Brunetti's methods were very on-brand for the Industrial Era, employing what scholar

Thomas Laquer called an "austere technological modernism."

Brunetti presided over multiple failed experiments, but those experiments represented "the beginning of a new era in the history of the dead body." After all, industrialized cremation machines are today the dominant mode of body disposal in almost every developed country.

The first corpse that Brunetti cremated was the body of a thirty-five-year-old woman placed in a brick furnace. The experiment was not unsuccessful, as the furnace did reduce her body down to five and a half pounds of bone chunks. But the method took too long for the professor's satisfaction — four hours.

Brunetti thought it might expedite the process to chop up the body pre-cremation. Corpse number two, a forty-five-year-old man, went into the same brick furnace in three layers: level one for limbs, level two for the head, chest, and pelvis, and level three for organs and other viscera. The cremation still took a frustrating four hours to complete, but now the bones that remained weighed only two and a half pounds.

Katrina has considered this tactic. Multiple composting experts have told her, "If you really want to compost efficiently you'd

159

chop up the body first." The unsettling suggestions from experts don't stop there. There are those who say she must add manure to the pile, and one avid composter who sent her an email reading, "Dear Ms. Spade, I am interested in your project. I have had excellent luck with my compost pile because I use leftover urine from hospitals. Have you considered that?"

"Did you write back?" I asked.

"I had to politely decline on the hospital urine. Is it a good source of nitrogen? Yes. Is it fast? Probably yes. Am I going to put a body into it? No."

Brunetti, undeterred by the thought of pulling the dead apart, decided in his next round of experiments to go hotter, putting various body parts into an altogether different furnace that produced coal gas, a substance used for electricity in the nineteenth century. This furnace was several hundred degrees hotter and took two hours longer (six hours total). But the end result was bones that were completely carbonized, zapped of all organic material. All traces of what made the human a human, including the DNA — though the professor would not have understood this at the time — were gone.

In his 1884 paper, Brunetti wrote of cremation:

It is a solemn, magnificent moment, which has a sacred, majestic quality. The combustion of a corpse always produced in me a very strong emotional arousal. As long as its shape is still human, and the flesh is burning, one is overcome by wonder, admiration; when the form has vanished, and all the body is charred, sadness takes over.

By 1873, Brunetti was ready to debut the results of his experiments at the Vienna World Exhibition. His booth, #54 in the Italian section, featured various glass cubes containing the results of his experiments — bones and flesh in varying degrees of disintegration.

Brunetti's cremation technology represented a chance for society to skip over decomposition and incinerate the body down to its inorganic material. He hoped to industrialize the process, to do it as quickly as possible with the efficiency of a factory line. According to Laquer, modern cremation, as Brunetti saw it, "was a problem for science and technology." The message was clear: nature, left to her own devices, was far too sloppy and inept, taking months to do what a 2,000-degree blast furnace could do in mere hours. A sign at Brunetti's booth at the Vienna exhibit read *"Vermibus erepti — Puro consumimur igni,"* or "Saved from the worms, consumed by the purifying flame."

Almost 150 years later, both Katrina and I would disagree with Brunetti that only flames can purify. The poet Walt Whitman spoke of soil and earth as the great transformers, accepting "the leavings" of men and producing "such divine materials." Whitman marveled at the ability of the earth to reabsorb the corrupt, the vile, the diseased, and produce new, pristine life. There is no reason to zap away your organic material with gas or flame when there is good to be done with "the leavings" of your mortal form.

Dr. J headed back down to the tent in the parking area to upload data from an electronic logger which had been placed on the chest of John Compost to record the temperature spikes his body experienced while in the mound. That left Katrina and me to start uncovering the second mound, containing June Compost. The seventy-eight-year-old woman was emaciated by disease at the time of her death. Her mound consisted of pure woodchips and was at the bottom of the hill, uncovered, in the shade.

As we got deeper into the pile, the dirt

exposed larval beetles and grubs. The soil inside the pile was abundant and dark — compost is often referred to as "black gold." But the presence of the insects was not ideal, as it meant there was still something inside the pile serving as a nutrition source, a feast to keep these creatures occupied. Then I hit June's femur, covered in a thick white leftover of decomposed fat, the consistency of Greek yogurt (apologies, Greek yogurt fans). As we uncovered more, we found the woman at the very end stages of decomposition, mostly down to bone.

June Compost's problems were the opposite of John Compost's. There was enough moisture (which is why she had been successfully taken down to bone), but without enough nitrogen the temperature in her mound never got high enough to reconfigure her bones to soil.

Neither John nor June Compost had been a success. But this was only the beginning of Katrina's experiments. More bodies will come into the FOREST facility to be composted. At Wake Forest University, a law professor named Tanya Marsh is assigning her cemetery law students to comb through state laws to discover how to legalize recomposition facilities in all fifty states. At Western Washington University, a soil scientist and composting expert, Lynne Carpenter-Boggs, will begin experiments with human-sized animals (small cows, large dogs, shorn sheep, the occasional pig — all predeceased). There are already studies underway on what the composting process does to mercury amalgam fillings in teeth, whose toxic release into the air is one of the biggest environmental concerns about cremation.

"Lynne called me on the phone the other day to talk about the teeth study," Katrina said, "and casually mentioned, 'I dug my own grave and slept in it last night.' She's a pretty serious practicing Sufi."

"Damn, dug her own grave and slept in it," I replied.

"Yeah, death is part of her spiritual practice. She's *much* more than just a lover of livestock composting."

It is worth noting that the main players in the recomposition project are women — scientists, anthropologists, lawyers, architects. Educated women, who have the privilege to devote their efforts to righting a wrong. They've given prominent space in their professional careers to changing the current system of death. Katrina noted that "humans are so focused on preventing aging and decay — it's become an obsession.

And for those who have been socialized female, that pressure is relentless. So decomposition becomes a radical act. It's a way to say, 'I love and accept myself.' "

I agree with Katrina here. Women's bodies are so often under the purview of men, whether it's our reproductive organs, our sexuality, our weight, our manner of dress. There is a freedom found in decomposition, a body rendered messy, chaotic, and wild. I relish this image when visualizing what will become of my future corpse.

When deathcare became an industry in the early twentieth century, there was a seismic shift in who was responsible for the dead. Caring for the corpse went from visceral, primeval work performed by women to a "profession," an "art," and even a "science," performed by well-paid men. The corpse, with all its physical and emotional messiness, was taken from women. It was made neat and clean, and placed in its casket on a pedestal, always just out of our grasp.

Maybe a process like recomposition is our attempt to reclaim our corpses. Maybe we wish to become soil for a willow tree, a rosebush, a pine — destined in death to both rot and nourish on our own terms.

Spain:
Barcelona

The American funeral home exhibits a suspiciously uniform aesthetic: squat mid-century brick, velvet-curtained interior, uneasy aroma of Glade plug-ins (covering over the antiseptic smells from the body preparation room). By contrast, the Altima funeral home, in Barcelona, is Google-headquarters-meets-Church-of-Scientology. It is minimalist, hypermodern, projecting the potential for cultlike activity. Its three stories feature floors, walls, and ceilings of elegant white stone. Wide balconies allow you to step outside and overlook the gardens. Not parking lots, *gardens.* One wall is floor-to-ceiling glass, exposing a panorama of the city stretching from the mountains to the sea. Stop by the espresso bar to take advantage of the free Wi-Fi.

The Mediterranean sun streamed through the window and reflected off the white floor. Blinded by the glare, I found myself in a perpetual cross-eyed squint during conversations with Altima's attractive, well-groomed employees, including Josep, the dashing man in a suit who ran the whole operation.

In addition to Josep, sixty-three people work at Altima's well-oiled facility. They pick up bodies, prepare them, file death certificates, meet with families, run funeral services. Altima handles almost one-quarter of all the deaths in Barcelona, which works out at ten to twelve bodies a day. Families choose between *sepultura* or *incinerar* (burial or cremation). Spain, thanks to its Catholic roots, has been slower to adopt cremation than most European countries; its cremation rate is at 35 percent, with urban Barcelona closer to 45 percent.

To understand the death rituals of Barcelona, you must understand glass. Glass means transparency, unclouded confrontation with the brutal reality of death. Glass also means a solid barrier. It allows you to come close but never quite make contact.

Altima boasts two large *oratorios* (chapels) and twenty family rooms. A family can rent one of these rooms and spend the entire day with their dead, showing up first thing in the morning and staying until the doors close at 10 p.m. And many families do. The

catch is that the entire time, the body will be behind glass.

You have options as to the manner of glass you'd prefer be placed between you and your loved one. If you select a Spanish-style viewing, Altima will display your loved one in their coffin, surrounded by flowers, behind one large pane of glass, akin to a department store window. If you prefer the Catalan-style, Josep and his team will slide the open coffin into a Snow White display case in the center of the room. Either way, Altima can maintain a steady temperature around the body of 0–6 degrees Celsius (32–42 degrees Fahrenheit).

Behind the scenes, there were long corridors where the bodies in wooden coffins awaited their big moment. Pint-sized *Alice in Wonderland* metal doors opened to allow Altima staff to slip the body into its display or glass casket.

"What makes the glass casket Catalan-style?" I inquired.

My interpreter was Jordi Nadal, head of the publishing company that released my first book in Spain. Jordi was a Zorba the Greek character, dropping *carpe diem*-themed bon mots at every opportunity, keeping your wine glass full and squid and paella on your plate.

"Our Catalan families want to be closer to the dead," was the answer.

"By putting them behind the glass like a zoo exhibit? What trouble are the corpses planning on causing, exactly?" is a thing I *did not* say.

The fact was, I had spent the whole week in Spain doing interviews with the national press on the ways modern funeral homes keep the family separated from the dead. Altima had read those interviews. That they had allowed me to make this visit at all was a miracle, and showed a willingness to engage on alternative methods that no American funeral corporation had ever shown me. I didn't want to push my luck.

That's not to say there wasn't any tension. One employee, an older gentleman, asked if I was enjoying my time in Barcelona.

"It is gorgeous, I don't want to leave. Perhaps I will stay here and apply for a job at Altima!" I said in jest.

"With your views we would not hire you," he joked back, not without a slight edge to his voice.

"Do you have this phrase in Spanish, 'Keep your friends close and enemies closer?' "

"Ah, yes." He raised his eyebrows. "We'll do that."

The people I spoke to in Barcelona (regular citizens and funeral workers alike) complained of how rushed the process of death seemed. Everyone felt the body should be buried within twenty-four hours, but nobody was quite sure why. Mourners felt pressure from funeral directors to get things completed. In turn, the funeral directors protested that families "want things fast, fast, fast, in less than twenty-four hours." Everyone seemed trapped in the twenty-four-hour hamster wheel. Theories for this time frame ranged from historical factors like Spain's Muslim past (Islam requires bodies to be buried swiftly after death) to the warm Mediterranean weather, which would allow bodies to putrefy more quickly than elsewhere in Europe.

Prior to the twentieth century, it was not uncommon to believe that the corpse was a dangerous entity that spread pestilence and disease. Imam Dr. Abduljalil Sajid explained to the BBC that the Muslim tradition of burial in the first twenty-four hours "was a way to protect the living from any sanitary issues." The Jewish tradition follows similar rules. Such fear across cultures inspired the developed world to erect protective barriers between the corpse and the family. The United States, New Zealand, and Canada embraced embalming, chemically preparing the body. Here in Barcelona they placed the body behind glass.

The shift toward removing those barriers has been slow-going, even though prominent entities like the World Health Organization make clear that even after a mass death event, "contrary to common belief, there is no evidence that corpses pose a risk of disease 'epidemics.' "

The Centers for Disease Control puts it even more bluntly: "The sight and smell of decay are unpleasant, but they do not create a public health hazard."

With this in mind, I asked Josep, the owner, if they would allow the family to keep the body at home, sans protective glass boxes. Though he insisted Altima rarely received such a request, Josep promised they would allow it, sending their employees out to the home to "close the holes."

We took a freight elevator downstairs and stepped into the body preparation area. In Spain, bodies are so swiftly sent off *sepultura* or *incinerar* that they are rarely embalmed. Altima did have an embalming room, with two metal tables, but they only perform full embalmings on bodies that are being transported to a different part of Spain or out of the country entirely. Unlike the United States, where aspiring embalmers must pursue the overkill combination of a mortuary school degree and an apprenticeship, in Spain all training is done inhouse, at the funeral home. Altima boasts of importing embalming experts from France to train their staff, "including the man who embalmed Lady Di!"

In the body prep room, two identical older women, in identical button-up sweaters with identical crucifixes around their necks, lay in identical wooden coffins. Two female Altima employees leaned over the first woman, blow-drying her hair. Two male employees leaned over the second, rubbing her face and hands with heavy cream. These bodies were on their way upstairs, destined to repose in glass coffins or behind glass walls.

I asked Jordi, my publisher, if he had ever seen dead bodies like this, without the glass barrier. With his typical verve, he allowed that although he hadn't, he was ready for the encounter. "Seeing the truth like this, is always elegant," he explained. "It gives you what you deserve as a human being. It gives you dignity."

Joan was a more salt-and-pepper version of his brother Josep. He ran Cementiri Parc Roques Blanques ("White Rocks"), one of Altima's cemeteries. All Spanish cemeteries are public, but private companies like Altima can contract to run them for a designated length of time. The electric golf cart buzzed up and down the rolling hills, passing above-ground mausoleums and columbaria. Roques Blanques resembled many American cemeteries, with bright bursts of flowers laid out on flat granite headstones.

One aspect, however, was drastically different. Joan radioed one of the cemetery's groundskeepers to join us at the top of a hill. There were no graves up here, just three discreet manhole covers. The groundskeeper bent down to unlock the heavy padlocks and slid back the metal circles. I squatted beside him and peeked in. Beneath the covers were deep holes carved into the hillside, filled to the top with bags of bones and piles of cremated remains.

Someone from North America might recoil at the idea of an idyllic cemetery harboring mass graves, filled with hundreds of sets of remains. But this was business as usual at this Spanish cemetery.

The dead at Roques Blanques start out in a ground grave, or in a wall mausoleum. But the dead haven't purchased a home at the cemetery as much as they have rented an apartment. They have a lease, and their time in the grave is limited.

Before a body is placed into a grave, the family must lease a minimum of five years' decomposition time. When the corpse has decayed down to bone, they will join their brethren in the communal pits, making way for the more recently deceased. The only exceptions are made for embalmed bodies (again, rare in Spain). Those bodies may need more like twenty years for their transition. Joan's crew will periodically peek in on embalmed bodies, and say, "Oh, okay, buddy — not done!" The corpse will have to stay in its grave or wall crypt until it is ready to join the collective bone club.

This "grave recycling" is not just a Spanish practice. It extends to most of Europe, again baffling the average North American, who views the grave as a permanent home. In Seville, in the south of Spain, they have almost no available cemetery land. The cremation rate there is 80 percent (very high for Spain), because the government subsidizes cremation down to a cost of only 60–80 euro. It is economically prudent to die in Seville.

Over in Berlin, German families rent graves for twenty to thirty years. Recently, the cemetery land has become not only prime real estate for the dead, but for the living. With so many choosing cremation, long-standing cemeteries are being converted into parks, community gardens, even children's playgrounds. This is a hard transition to reconcile. Cemeteries are beautiful spaces of cultural, historical, and community value. By the same token, they possess great cultural and restorative potential, as this Public Radio International piece reported:

Then there's the Berlin graveyard, mostly cleared of headstones, that is now a community garden, including a small Syrian refugee garden with tomatoes, onions, and mint.

The old tombstone carver's workshop at

the entrance to the graveyard now hosts German language classes for refugees.

"It's a space that's been abandoned, and used for burying people, used for, now, gardening and cultivating human beings in the best way possible," said Fetewei Tarekegn, the head gardener of the community project.

Roques Blanques is attempting to do more than just bury the dead. They have won awards for their green initiatives. Their fleet of vehicles is electric, including the hearse shaped like a silver bug, conceived by students at a Barcelona design school. The ten hectares of land lodge protected squirrel colonies, wild boars, and special houses for bats. The bat colonies are cultivated to control the dangerous invasion of the Asian tiger mosquito, although Roques Blanques received some bad press for daring to associate their cemetery with bats, vampires, the vile undead!

Environmentally sound though these initiatives may be, Roques Blanques is not a natural cemetery. The dead are required to be buried in wooden coffins in granite crypts, stacked in layers of two, three, or six people. This is puzzling. Why not place the body directly into the soil, without granite?

This would allow the bones to decompose completely, meaning there would be no need for the communal grave space, thus freeing up the land. "We just don't do that in Spain," Joan said.

Joan has decided to be cremated, but seemed to understand the contradiction in that choice. "It takes nine months to create a baby, but we destroy the body too easily through industrial cremation processes." He thought for a moment. "The body should take the same nine-month time to disintegrate." I whispered to Jordi, "It sounds like he wants natural burial!"

Spain is very good at being *almost* green in its postmortem ideas. On our tour we passed through a grove of trees, Mediterranean and native to this area, of course. Roques Blanques will plant a tree and bury five sets of your family's ashes around it, making it a literal family tree. They are the first cemetery in Spain to offer this option.

Roques Blanques's "family tree" is similar to the wildly popular biodegradable urn, Bios Urn, created by a design firm in Barcelona. You might have seen it floating through your social media feed. Bios Urn resembles a large McDonald's cup filled with soil, a tree seed, and a place for cremated remains. One of the most popular

articles on the Bios Urn is called "This Awesome Urn Will Turn You into a Tree After You Die!"

It is a lovely thought, and a tree may grow from the soil provided, but after the 1,800-degree cremation process, the remaining bones are reduced to inorganic, basic carbon. With everything organic (including DNA) burned away, your sterile ashes are way past being useful to plants or trees.

There are nutrients, but their combination is all wrong for plants, and don't contribute to ecological cycles. Bios Urn charges $145 for one of their urns. The symbolism is beautiful. But symbolism does not make you part of the tree.

Roques Blanques has two cremation retorts (machines) at the cemetery, which cremate 2,600 people every year. Walking in to see the machines, I was surprised by two men in suits flanking a light wooden coffin with a cross emblem, waiting with hands folded outside a preheated retort. "Oh, you're waiting for us, excellent! *Gracias!*" I am always excited to witness a cremation. It never gets old, no matter how many you've overseen or performed. It is powerful to be in the presence of a corpse mere moments from being transformed by fire.

Joan took us on a brief tour of the cremation room, including the fifteen-year-old cremation machine used for family-witnessed cremations. It was significantly nicer than the industrial warehouses back home. "The walls are marble from Italy, the floor is granite from Brazil," he explained.

"Sixty percent of our families come to witness the cremation," Joan announced. Here's where my jaw hit the polished granite floor.

"I'm sorry, 60 percent?" I reeled.

That is an enormous number — far higher than the percentage in the United States, where many families don't even know they have the option of witnessing the cremation.

Before the cremation began, Joan brought us just outside the room, behind — are you ready for it? — three panes of glass stretching floor to ceiling. They were identical to the three panes of glass that had separated us from the body at the funeral home. "Why do you use the glass for cremations?" I asked Joan.

"The angle is such that you can't see fully inside the oven, to the flames," he replied.

It was true. Try as I might, I couldn't quite see the fire, just the edge of the cremation machine. The two men slid the coffin into the brick-lined machine. When the heavy metal door came down, they pulled a classy wooden door across the front of the retort, hiding the machine's industrial façade.

Barcelona was the land of almost. They had initiatives for eco-cemeteries, animal conservation, and the growth of native trees. Their bodies were not embalmed, and were buried in wooden coffins. *Almost* a green burial, except for the granite fortress the coffin was required to be placed in. They had witness cremations that 60 percent of families attended, and funeral homes in which the family could stay the whole day with their loved one. *Almost* a paragon of family interaction at death, yet there was glass separating the family from the body at the viewing and at the cremation, setting up Mom as a museum exhibit.

I wanted to be self-righteous about the use of glass, but couldn't, for this simple reason: with its elegant marble and glass, Altima had provided the one thing the United States needs more than anything — butts in the seats. People showed up for death here. They showed up for daylong viewings, sitting close vigil with the body. They showed up for witness cremations: 60 percent at this location. Perhaps the barrier of glass was the training wheels required to let a death-wary public get close, but not too close.

The cremation process would take approximately ninety minutes. Joan took Jordi, my publisher, to the back of the machine, where the family does not come. Pulling open a hinged metal window, he allowed us to peer inside the cremation chamber. Fierce blasts of fire shot down from the ceiling and devoured the top of the coffin. Jordi's eyes widened as he took his turn peek-

ing in, his pupils reflecting the flames.

For his trouble in showing me around Barcelona, poor Jordi had been rewarded with multiple close encounters with the dead. As we ate what seemed like a fourteen-course dinner in the city, I inquired what the day had been like for him. He thought, and replied that "when your bills come due, you have to pay them. At my company, I pay my bills. Here at this restaurant, I pay my bill. It is the same with feelings. When the feelings come, the fear of death, I must feel those feelings. I must pay my bill. It is being alive."

JAPAN:
TOKYO

Tokudane!, the Japanese morning television show, cut to a commercial break. Women in grape suits danced to a pulsing electronic beat. Animated bunnies clipped a toupee onto an astounded man's head. *Tokudane!* returned and the hosts introduced the next segment, which began with a white-robed monk praying in a temple. There were flowers and incense; he appeared to be presiding over a funeral.

The temple was crammed with distraught mourners. The image pulled back to reveal the altar and the source of all this sorrow — nineteen robotic dogs. The camera zoomed in on their broken paws and snapped-off tails. I watched the TV at the hotel breakfast buffet in rapt attention, eating fried eggs shaped like hearts.

Electronics giant Sony released the Aibo ("companion" in Japanese) in 1999. The three-and-a-half-pound robocanine had the ability to learn and respond based on its owner's commands. Adorable and charming, the Aibo also barked, sat, and mimicked peeing. Their owners claimed the pups helped combat loneliness and health issues. Sony discontinued the Aibo in 2006, but promised to keep making repairs. Then, in 2014, they discontinued repairs as well, a harsh mortality lesson for the owners of the roughly 150,000 Aibos sold. A cottage industry of robotic vets and online grief support forums sprang up, culminating in funerals for Aibos tragically beyond repair.

Once the *Tokudane!* segment ended, I headed into Tokyo full of heart-shaped eggs to meet my interpreter, Emily (Ayako) Sato. She had suggested we meet at the statue of Hachikō in the Shibuya railway station. Hachikō is a national hero in Japan. Hachikō was also a dog (a real one). In the 1930s he would meet his owner, an agriculture professor, at the rail station each day after work. One day, the professor never came to meet Hachikō; he had died of a brain hemorrhage. Undeterred, Hachikō returned to the station every day for the next nine years, when his own death halted the ritual. Dogs are a solid meeting point from a cross-cultural perspective. Everyone respects a devoted canine.

Sato-san was waiting when I arrived, a woman in late middle age who did not look a day over forty. She wore a power pantsuit and sensible walking shoes. "My secret is walking ten thousand steps each day." I almost lost her several times as we descended into the labyrinthine bowels of the Shibuya station, swept up in the throngs of Tokyo's well-dressed denizens. "Perhaps I need to hold up one of those flags that tour group leaders carry, with a skull on it, just for you," she grinned.

After two turnstiles, three staircases, and four escalators, we reached our platform. "We're safer down here from earthquakes," Sato-san announced. This wasn't a non sequitur. Just that day there had been a 6.8 magnitude earthquake off the coast. I couldn't speak to anyone in Tokyo without them referencing the psychological impact of the 2011 earthquake, with its subsequent tsunami that roared through northeast Japan and killed more than 15,000 people.

On the subway platform, sliding glass barriers separated the riders from the rails below. "Those barriers are somewhat new," Sato-san explained. "For one thing they prevent" — she lowered her voice — "the suicides." Japan's rate of death by suicide is one of the highest in the developed world.

185

Sato-san continued, "Unfortunately, the workers have become very efficient in cleaning up the train suicides, collecting the body parts and whatnot."

In the Judeo-Christian view — and thus, the dominant Western view — to die by suicide is a sinful, selfish act. This perception has been slow to fade, though the science is clear that suicide has root causes in diagnosable mental disorders and substance abuse. ("Sin" does not qualify for the DSM-5.)

The cultural meaning of suicide in Japan is different. It's viewed as a selfless, even honorable act. The samurai introduced the practice of *seppuku,* literally "cutting the abdomen," self-disembowelment by sword to prevent capture by the enemy. In World War II, nearly 4,000 men died as *kamikaze* pilots, turning their planes into missiles and crashing into enemy ships. Apocryphal but famous legends tell of the practice of *uba-*

sute, where elderly women were carried on their sons' backs into the forest to be abandoned in times of famine. The woman would stay dutifully put, succumbing to hypothermia or starvation.

Outsiders say that the Japanese romanticize suicide, and that Japan has a "suicide culture." But the reality is more complicated. The Japanese view of self-inflicted death as altruistic is more about wanting not to be a burden, rather than about fascination with mortality itself. Furthermore, "foreign scholars can look at statisti-

cal numbers on suicide, but they will not understand the phenomenon," argues writer Kenshiro Ohara. "Only Japanese people can understand the suicide of the Japanese."

For me, observing death in Japan was like gazing through the looking glass: everything familiar but distorted. Like America, Japan is a developed nation, where funerals and cemeteries are big business. Large funeral corporations play a sizable role in both Western and Japanese markets. Their pristine facilities are staffed by professional death workers. If that were the whole story, it would have made no sense for me to visit. But that is not the whole story.

Koukokuji Buddhist temple, a seventeenth-century building tucked away off a quiet street in Tokyo, is home to a modest cemetery, with aged headstones representing generations of families that have come to worship here. A black and white cat lounged on the stone path. We stepped out of modern Tokyo and into a Miyazaki movie. Yajima jūshoku (*jūshoku* means head priest or monk) emerged to greet us, an affable man in a brown robe with close-cropped white hair and glasses.

In contrast to his archaic surroundings, Yajima jūshoku is a man of new ideas, specifically, how to memorialize cremated remains (my kind of guy). Funeral directors in the United States blanch with fear at the thought of a national "cremation culture," which would undercut profit margins in embalming and casket sales. In reality, we have no idea what a homogenous "cremation culture" might look like. But the Japanese do. They have a cremation rate of 99.9 percent — the highest in the world. No other country even comes close (sorry, Taiwan: 93 percent; and Switzerland: 85 percent).

The emperor and empress were the final holdouts, still choosing full body burial. But several years ago, Emperor Akihito and his wife Empress Michiko announced they would also be cremated, breaking with four hundred years of royal burial tradition.

When Koukokuji Temple reached capacity, the priest Yajima could have invested in an old-fashioned cemetery space. Instead, seven years ago he built the Ruriden columbarium. (Columbaria are separate buildings for storing cremated remains.) "Buddhism has always been state-of-the-art," he explained. "It is quite natural to use technology alongside Buddhism. I see no conflict at all." With that, he showed us through the doors of the complex's newest hexagonal building.

We stood in the darkness while Yajima punched something into a keypad at the entrance. Moments later, two thousand floor-to-ceiling Buddhas began to glow and pulse a vivid blue. "Woooaahhh," Sato-san and I bleated in unison, stunned and delighted. I had seen photographs of Ruriden, but to be surrounded, 360 degrees, by the luminous Buddhas was overwhelming.

Yajima opened a locked door, and we peeked behind the Buddha walls at six hundred sets of bones. "Labeled to make it easy to find Miss Kubota-san," he smiled. Each set of cremated remains corresponded to a crystal Buddha on the wall.

When a family member comes to visit Ruriden, they either type in the name of the deceased or pull out a smart card with a chip, similar to the cards used on Tokyo's subways. After the family keys in at the entrance, the walls light up blue, except for one single Buddha shimmering clear white. No need to squint through names trying to find Mom — the white light will guide you straight to her.

"All of this evolved," said Yajima. "For example, we started with a touch pad, where you type in your family member's name. One day I saw a very old woman struggling to type a name in, so that's when we got the smart cards. She just had to tap the card and can immediately find her dead person!"

Yajima headed back to the keypad controller, and instructed us to stand in the center of the room. "The autumn scene!" he announced, and the formation of Buddhas turned yellow and brown with shifting red patches, like piles of freshly fallen leaves. "Winter scene!" and the Buddhas turned to snowdrifts of light blue and white. "Shooting star!" and the Buddhas turned purple as white spots jumped from Buddha to Buddha, like a stop-motion animation of the night sky.

The majority of columbaria leave no room for innovation. Their design is the same the world over. Endless rows of granite walls, where ashes reside behind the etched names of the dead. If individuality is a priority, you may be allowed to affix a small picture, a stuffed bear, or a bouquet of flowers.

This LED light show could have been a Disney production, but there was something in the sophisticated design of the lights that made it feel as though I were being swaddled in a Technicolor womb.

"The afterlife of Buddhism is filled with treasures and light," Yajima explained.

Religious scholars John Ashton and Tom

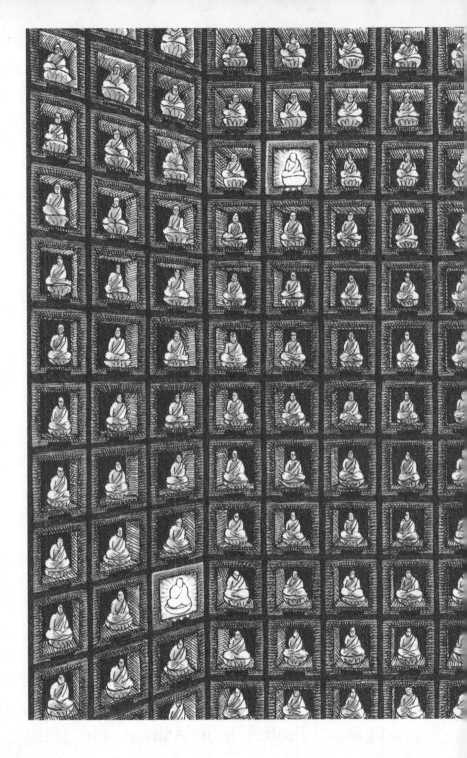

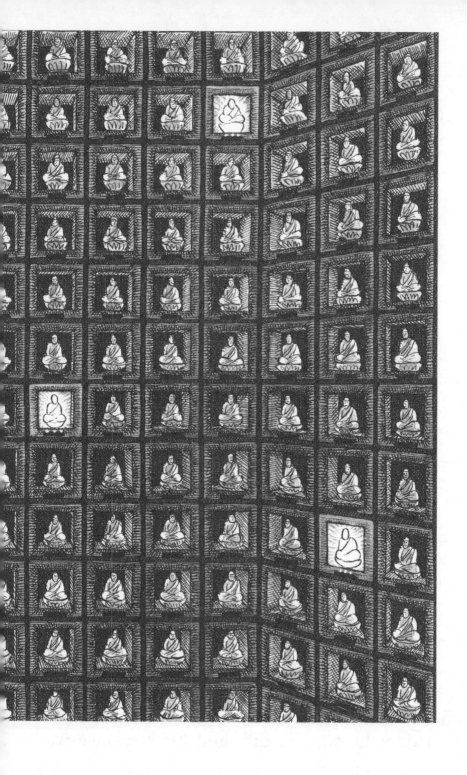

Whyte described the Pure Land (the celestial realm of East Asian Buddhism) as "decorated with jewels and precious metals and lined with banana and palm trees. Cool refreshing ponds and lotus flowers abound and wild birds sing the praises of the Buddha three times a day."

In designing Ruriden, Yajima was creating "an afterlife along the path of Buddha."

The Buddha lights weren't always this elaborate. One of the early visitors to the new facility at Ruriden was a light designer, and she volunteered to create the scenes from different seasons. "At first, the lights looked like a Las Vegas show!" Yajima laughed. "This is not a toy, I said! Too much! We canceled that. As natural as possible, I said. The work is still happening to create that atmosphere, as natural as possible."

Yajima invited us for tea inside the temple and offered me a stool, brought out for visiting foreigners. He believed I couldn't endure sitting cross-legged on the floor mats for the duration of tea and conversation. I assured him I absolutely could. (I couldn't. My legs fell painfully asleep within the first three minutes.)

I asked Yajima why he had designed Ruriden the way he did, and his response was impassioned. "We had to act, we had to do something. Japan has fewer children. Japanese people are living longer. The family is supposed to look after your grave, but we don't have enough people to look after everyone's grave. We had to do something for those people left behind."

A full quarter of Japan's population is over the age of sixty-five. That, combined with a low birthrate, has caused Japan's population to shrink by one million people in the last five years. Japanese women have the longest life expectancy in the world; Japanese men have the third longest. More importantly, their "healthy life expectancy" (not just old, but old and independent) is the longest for both genders. As the population ages, the need for nurses and caregivers is swelling. People in their seventies are caring for people in their nineties.

My interpreter, Sato-san, knows this well. She herself is responsible for the care of six people — her parents, her husband's parents, and two uncles. All are in their mideighties or early nineties. A few months ago, her great aunt died at one hundred and two.

This army of the elderly (the "silver market") worked their whole lives, saved money, and had few if any children. They have money to burn. The *Wall Street Journal* said that "one of Japan's hottest business buzzwords has become *'shūkatsu'* or 'end of life,' referring to the explosion of products and services aimed at people preparing for their final years."

Revenues in the Japanese death industry have increased by 335 billion yen (3 billion US dollars) since the year 2000. A company called Final Couture markets designer shrouds and specialized photographers create end-of-life portraits to be displayed at funerals.

People show up years in advance to purchase their Buddhas at Ruriden. Yajima encourages them to visit often and pray for others, and thereby face their own death. When they die, "they will be welcomed by the people who went to Buddha before you."

Then there are those who do not plan ahead, who have no close family. Their bodies leave dismal reddish-brown outlines on carpets or bedspreads when they are not found for weeks or months after death. They are victims of Japan's epidemic of *kodokushi,* or "lonely deaths": elderly people who die isolated and alone, with no one to find their bodies, let alone to come pray at their graves. There are even specialized companies hired by landlords to clean what is left behind after a *kodokushi.*

When Yajima built Ruriden, he "thought of the man who doesn't have any children and says, 'What will I do, who will pray for me?' "

Each morning, Yajima enters Ruriden and punches in the day's date. That morning he punched in May 13. Several Buddhas glowed yellow, representing the people who had died on that day. Yajima lit incense and prayed for them. He remembers them, even if there is no family left to do so. For an elderly man or woman with no remaining family, the glowing Buddhas at Ruriden will act as their afterlife community.

Yajima jūshoku may be a powerful priest, but he is also a designer. "When I pray, I also think about creating. How do we create something new, filled with dazzling light? How do we create new Buddhas?"

For him, the act of prayer is essential to creativity. "Every time I pray, the different ideas pop up. . . . I'm not a man who sits at a desk to create a plan. It's all while I'm praying."

What if Ruriden fills up with ashes? "If it fills up then I will consider a second or third." Yajima smiled. "I'm already thinking of them."

In the early twentieth century, Japan's privately operated crematories were (at least in the eyes of the press) dens of iniquity. The men who operated the crematories were rumored to steal gold teeth from the dead. Even stranger, they were said to steal body parts, which were then processed into medicines purported to cure syphilis. The machines still burned wood instead of gas, which made the process a lengthy one. The family had to leave the crematory and return home while the body burned overnight. Historian Andrew Bernstein explained that "as a precaution against the theft of body parts, gold teeth, jewelry, or articles of clothing, mourners were given keys to the individual ovens, which they had to bring back to the crematory to recover the bones and ashes," like lockers at a bus station.

The Mizue Funeral Hall, founded as a public crematory in 1938, introduced a more modern approach. The machines used fuel, allowing the families to handle everything in one day (no keys necessary). Advocates argued that crematories should be rebranded "funeral centers" and placed in gardenlike settings as a form of "aesthetic management." Eighty years later, the Mizue Funeral Hall continues to operate, and still benefits from "aesthetic management." The sprawling complex abuts a river to the west, gardens and a playground to the south, and a junior high and two elementary schools to the east.

Like Mizue, Rinkai, the crematory I visited, offers the full death experience. That day, four separate funeral halls were set up, with funerals staggered throughout the day. Private funeral company employees arrived long before the families with flower wreaths and other swag add-ons to decorate the room: bamboo, plants, glowing orbs (I was most impressed by the glowing orbs). Social anthropologist Hikaru Suzuki explained that in modern Japan (as in the West) "professionals prepare, arrange, and conduct commercial funeral ceremonies, leaving the bereaved only the fees to pay."

One of Suzuki's interview subjects, an eighty-four-year-old man, bemoaned the loss of ritual around death. In the 1950s, he complained, everyone knew exactly what to do when someone died; they didn't need to *pay* someone to help them. "Look at young people today in the presence of death," he said. "The first thing they do is call a funeral company. They act like helpless children. Such an embarrassing situation never arose in the past." The truly shocking part, his wife chimed in, is that "young people today don't seem to be embarrassed about it either." So not only do the young have zero death literacy, they don't seem to mind.

Of course, the younger generations raise their eyebrows at the superstitions of the old. The same man admitted that his grand-daughter (a medical student) made fun of him when he hearkened back to funerals past, where "when a woman was pregnant she wasn't allowed to go near the deceased. It was said that if a cat jumped over the deceased's head, the evil spirit of the animal would go into the corpse and make the body rise up." To prevent the corpse from trans-forming into an evil cat zombie, well, "the cat was kept away from the dead . . ."

Each of the four halls at Rinkai was set up for the funeral of a different elderly woman. Digital photo frames with portraits of the women were placed at the front of the hall near the casket. In her portrait, Mrs. Fumi wore a blue sweater over a white collared shirt.

In a tiny side room, Mrs. Tanaka lay un-embalmed in a lavender cremation casket, dry ice* tucked around her body to keep her chilled. Her family surrounded her, their heads bowed. Her funeral would be held from 10 a.m. to noon the next day, directly followed by the cremation.

The old men assembled in a separate room, smoking, segregated from the general grievers. "I remember funeral halls before the smoking rooms," Sato-san told me. "Mixing the cigarette smoke with the funeral incense was terrible."

The crematory itself, where the bodies were taken after their funerals, was like the foyer of a fancy New York office building, everything made of imposing dark granite. This was the shiny new Lexus to America's old Dodge pickup truck. Ten cremation machines were hidden behind ten silver doors, meticulously polished free of smudges. Grey stainless steel conveyor belts deposited the dead into each machine. It was cleaner and sleeker than any crematory I had ever seen.

Prices were posted outside the crematory: to cremate an unborn baby cost 9,000 yen, a single body part 7,500 yen, 2,000 yen to divide up the bones of a grown person into separate urns. Also posted was a list of items

* *Not* the rolling fog eighties music video type.

201

the family was not allowed to cremate alongside their dead loved one, including but not limited to cellphones, golf balls, dictionaries, large stuffed animals, Buddha figures made of metal, and watermelons.

"Wait, watermelons, really?"

"That's what it says!" Sato-san shrugged.

Three or so close family members, including the chief mourner (most likely the husband or eldest son), accompany a body into the crematory, and watch it glide into the machine. The family does not watch the cremation process itself, but instead joins the reception upstairs. When the cremation is complete, they continue past the crematory to three rooms designated for the *kotsuage.*

After the cremation, a fragmented (but complete) skeleton is pulled from the machine. Western crematories pulverize these bones into powdery ash, but the Japanese traditionally do not. The family walks into the *shūkotsu-shitsu,* or ash/bone collecting room, where the skeleton of their loved one awaits.

The family are handed pairs of chopsticks, one made of bamboo, one made of metal. The chief mourner begins with the feet, picking up bones with the chopsticks and placing them in the urn. Other family members join in and continue up the skeleton. The skull will not fit into the urn intact, so the cremator might intervene to break it up into smaller bone fragments using a metal chopstick. The final bone, the hyoid (the horseshoe-shaped bone underneath the jaw) is placed in the urn last.

In *People Who Eat Darkness,* a brilliant nonfiction account of two women murdered in Tokyo in the 1990s, Richard Lloyd Parry describes the funeral of an Australian named Carita Ridgway. Her parents had flown in to arrange for the funeral of their daughter, and were outsiders to the *kotsuage* custom.

> . . . they made the long drive to the crematorium on the outer edges of suburban Tokyo. They said goodbye to Carita, who lay peacefully in a coffin full of rose petals, and watched her disappear behind the steel doors of the furnace. None of them was prepared for what came next. After a pause, they were led into a room on the other side of the building, and each given a pair of white gloves and chopsticks. In the room, on a steel sheet, were Carita's remains, as they had emerged from the heat of the furnace. The incineration was incomplete. Wood, cloth, hair and

flesh had burned away, but the biggest bones, of legs and arms, as well as the skull, were cracked but recognisable. Rather than a neat box of ashes, the Ridgways were confronted with Carita's calcined skeleton; as the family, their task, a traditional part of every Japanese cremation, was to pick up her bones with the chopsticks and place them in the urn. "Rob [her boyfriend] couldn't handle it at all," Nigel [her father] said. "He thought we were monsters, even to think of it. But, perhaps it's because we were the parents, and she was our daughter . . . It sounds macabre, as I tell you about it now, but it didn't feel that way at the time. It was something emotional. It almost made me feel calmer. I felt as if we were looking after Carita."

The *kotsuage* was not part of the Ridgway family's culture, yet at the most difficult time in their lives it gave them a meaningful task to complete for Carita.

Not all of the bones may fit in the urn. Depending on the region of Japan where Mom was cremated, the family might take the remaining bone and ash home in a separate smaller bag, or leave it behind at the crematory. The crematory staff pulver-

izes the leftover bones and places them in sacks, then piles the sacks out of public view. When the pile is large enough, the pulverized bones are picked up by another specialized group, the ash collectors. From there they are placed in large graves in the mountains, eight by ten feet and over twenty feet deep. According to the sociologist Hikaru Suzuki, the ash collectors plant cherry trees and conifers atop the ash pits. "These cherry trees attract many visitors, but few of them recognize the secret of the trees' beauty."

Cherry groves offer a more elegant solution than the old method. In the past, the ashes would simply be buried on crematory property. But with the rise of fancier, park-like complexes such as Mizue Funeral Hall, the "dumping the bones out back" idea fell out of favor. Suzuki heard this group of ash collectors referred to as the *haibutsu kaishūsha,* or literally "person who collects trash." According to her, the cremators "look down on ash collectors for being mere manual laborers who have no responsibility for the spirit of the deceased." Having to deal with the corpse and the family is what makes a crematory employee "professional."

This was a strange distinction, between the cremators and the ash collectors. In my years cremating, those two jobs were one and the same. The body goes into the machine as a corpse, and comes out as bones and ash. In the West, where there is no *kotsuage,* families suffer great anxiety that they might receive the wrong set of ashes. They obsess over the question, "Is that really my mother in the urn?"* After a cremation, I attempt to remove every last fragment of bone or ash from the cremation machine. Nevertheless, some shards of bone fall into the cracks, and are eventually collected into bags. In California, we scatter

---

* Yes, it's her.

those bags at sea. I am both cremator and ash collector, both "professional" and "collector of trash."

When Sōgen Kato turned 111 years old in 2010, he became the oldest man in Tokyo. Officials came to his house to congratulate Kato on this impressive milestone. Kato's daughter would not let them in, alternately claiming that Kato was in a persistent vegetative state or that he was attempting to practice *sokushinbutsu,* the ancient art of self-mummification of Buddhist monks.

After repeated attempts, the police forcibly entered the home and found Kato's body, which had been dead for at least thirty years and was long since mummified (but still wearing his underwear). Instead of honoring her father and bringing him to the grave, Mr. Kato's daughter had locked his body in a room on the first floor of the family home. His granddaughter was quoted as saying, "My mother said, 'Leave him in there,' and he was left as he was." Over the years his eighty-one-year-old daughter pocketed over $100,000 of his pension payments.

What Kato-san's family did was astounding, not only for the length of their scam but because it demonstrated how much the

Japanese view of the dead body had changed. Traditionally, the corpse was seen as impure. Since the body was polluted, the family was expected to be active in performing rituals to purify and reset the body to a more benign and nonthreatening state — *imiake,* or "lifting of pollution."

To someone alive today, the list of rituals once performed to decontaminate both the living and the dead might seem endless. A list of highlights: drink sake before and after any contact with the body; light incense and candles so that the fire can cast out contamination; stay awake with the body all night, so no malevolent spirits enter the corpse; scrub your hands with salt after a cremation.

By the mid-twentieth century more people began to die in hospitals, away from the home. More professionals in charge meant the Japanese lost the sense that the dead body was impure. Cremation rose from 25 percent (at the turn of the century) to almost 100 percent. People felt contamination could be avoided by sending the corpse into the flames. The same shift occurred in the United States, but had the opposite result. It is disheartening that in the U.S., the professionalization of deathcare led to a greater fear of the body than ever before.

Again, a gaze through the looking glass.

In Yokohama, Japan's second largest city, you'll find Lastel, a portmanteau of Last + Hotel, as in, the last hotel you'll ever stay in . . . because you're dead. It's a hotel for corpses. The manager of Lastel, Mr. Tsuruo, didn't lead us through cobwebs by candlelight, as you might expect the proprietor of a corpse hotel to do. He was funny and outgoing, passionate about the facility and what it provides. By the end of my visit, I was whispering into my audio recorder, "I want it I want a corpse hotel *I want one.*"

Mr. Tsuruo led us into the elevator. "This elevator is not for the public, of course," he apologized. "Just for the stretcher and the workers." The elevator looked so clean you could eat off the floor. We exited on the sixth floor, where Lastel had a refrigerated storage room that held up to twenty dead bodies.

"I wanted something here that other facilities don't have," Mr. Tsuruo explained, as an electric stretcher shot down a metal track, floated underneath a white casket, lifted the casket from the rack, and delivered it to us at the entrance.

The walls were lined with casket-sized metal doors. "Where do they lead?" I asked.

Mr. Tsuruo motioned us to follow. We

entered a small room with incense, some couches. There was an identical set of small metal doors in this room, though they were better-disguised. A door opened, and in slid the white casket.

We continued into three different family rooms, where if you are a relative, you can come at any time of the day (the body is there, on average, for about four days) and call up the body from refrigerated storage. Your family member will be in the casket, their features lightly put into place (with no embalming) and dressed in a Buddhist costume or a more modern suit. "Maybe you can't make the funeral," Mr. Tsuruo said, "maybe you're working during the day, so you come by to visit and sit with the body."

One of the family rooms was larger, with big comfy couches, a television, and copious bouquets of flowers. It was a place to hang out with the dead, in comfort, with none of the strict time limits imposed by an American funeral home.

"It is 10,000 yen ($85) more to use this big room," he said.

"Worth it!" I replied.

To have that period to visit the body as often as you like, no reservations needed, seemed graceful and civilized. Antithetical to the "you paid for two hours in the viewing room and you'll get two hours in the viewing room" rules of a Western funeral home.

On another of Lastel's nine floors was a bathing room, bright clean and white. There was a tall, elegant washing station for "the last bath on this Earth." The traditional *yukan* bathing ceremony has, in recent years, been revived and performed commercially for close family members. The president of one company reintroducing the service said, "The bathing ceremony should [help] fill the psychological void in contemporary funeral ceremonies," because quickly taking the body away "does not offer sufficient time for the bereaved to contemplate death."

In my practice as a mortician I've found that both cleaning the body and spending time with it serves a powerful role in processing grief. It helps mourners see the corpse not as a cursed object, but as a beautiful vessel that once held their loved one. Famed Japanese home organizer Marie Kondo expresses a similar idea in her mega-bestseller *The Life-Changing Magic of Tidying Up*. Instead of purging everything into a garbage bag, she suggests you spend time with each item and "thank it for its service" before letting it go. Some critics found it silly to thank an ill-fitting sweater for its service, but the impulse actually comes from a profound place. Each separation is a small death, and should be honored. This concept is reflected in the Japanese relationship with the dead body. You don't just let Mother disappear into the cremation machine; you sit with her, and thank her body — and her — for her service as your mother. Only then do you let her go.

Mr. Tsuruo continued our tour by walking us down a cobblestone street, in actuality just a hallway in the Lastel building. The vibe was Victorian-themed Christmas display at the local shopping center. At the end of the hall was the front door of the "house." Mr. Tsuruo offered us tiny covers to put over our shoes.

"This is the 'living room type' family funeral," he said, opening the door into a normal Japanese condominium (sadly not Victorian-themed like the hallway).

"So this is just someone's condo? But no one actually stays here?" I asked, confused.

"Yes, they stay here. You can have the whole wake with the body here."

The condo had everything to make a family comfortable — microwaves, a big shower, sofas. Futon mats were available for up to fifteen people to sleep on overnight. In a big city like Yokohama, actual family apartments are not large enough to accommodate out-of-town mourners, so the family can gather here to hang out with the body instead.

This room flooded me with emotion and inspiration. There is a difficult discussion that rarely happens among American funeral directors: viewing the embalmed body is often an unpleasant experience for the family. There are exceptions to this rule, but the immediate family is given almost no meaningful time with the body (which in all likelihood was swiftly removed after death). Before the family has time to be with their dead person and process the loss, coworkers and distant cousins arrive, and everyone is forced into a public performance of grief and humility.

I wondered what it would be like if there were places like Lastel in every major city. Spaces outside the stiff, ceremonial norm, where the family can just be with the body, free from the performance required at a formal viewing. Spaces that are safe, comfortable, like home.

History is filled with ideas that arrived before their time. In the 1980s, Hiroshi Ueda, a Japanese camera company employee, created the first camera "extender stick," allowing him to capture self-portraits on his travels. The camera extender received a patent in 1983, but didn't sell. The contraption seemed so trivial that it even made a cameo in the book of *chindōgu* or "unuseful inventions." (Other *chindōgu:* tiny slippers for your cat, electric fans attached to chopsticks to cool off your ramen noodles.) Without fanfair, Ueda's patent expired in 2003. Today, surrounded by the masses wielding selfie sticks like narcissistic Jedi knights, he seemed remarkably calm in his defeat, telling the BBC, "We call it a 3 a.m. invention — it arrived too early."

The history of death and funerals is also filled with ideas before their time — the Reaper's own 3 a.m. inventions. One such creation arrived in 1820s' London. The city was at that time hunting for a solution to the problem of its overcrowded and smelly urban graveyards. Stacks of coffins went twenty feet deep into the soil. Half-decomposed bodies were exposed to public view when wood from their coffins was smashed up and sold to the poor for firewood. This overcrowding was so visible to the average Londoner that Reverend John Blackburn said, "Many delicate minds must sicken to witness the heaped soil, saturated and blackened with human remains and fragments of the dead." It was time to try something else.

Proposals to reform London's system of burials began to pour in, including one from an architect named Thomas Willson. If land shortage was the problem, Willson proposed that instead of digging further down to bury the bodies, London should send its dead skyward in a massive burial pyramid. This pyramid would be made from brick and granite and situated at the top of a hill — what is now Primrose Hill, overlooking central London. It would be ninety-four stories tall, four times taller than St. Paul's Cathedral, and hold five million bodies. I'm going to hit you with that number again: *five million bodies.*

The pyramid would sit on only eighteen acres of land, but would be able to hold the equivalent of 1,000 acres of bodies. Willson's Giant Corpse Pyramid (the actual name was the impossibly cool Metropolitan Sepulchre) spoke to Londoners' enthusiasm for Egyptian artifacts and architecture. Willson was even invited to present his idea before Parliament. And yet, the public did not embrace the concept. The *Literary Gazette* labeled the project a "monstrous piece of folly." The public wanted garden cemeteries, they wanted to push the dead outside the cramped churchyards of central London and send them to sprawling landscapes where they could picnic and commune with the dead. They didn't want a giant death mound (whose weight might have crushed the hill), a monument to rot, dominating the city's skyline.

All ended in shame for Willson. His pyramid idea was pilfered by a French architect. After accusing his colleague of intellectual theft, he was sued for libel. But what if the idea for the Metropolitan Sepulchre was just the selfie stick of mortality, arrived before its time? Every giant leap we take to redesign deathcare comes with the caveat that the

idea might end up in the pile with other *chindōgu.*

Just five minutes from the Ryōgoku station, right around the corner from the Sumo Hall in Tokyo, is one of the highest-tech funeral facilities in the world. On your lunch break you can hop on the train, walk past the wrestlers in their patterned kimonos, and arrive at Daitokuin Ryōgoku Ryoen, a multistory temple and graveyard.

Daitokuin Ryōgoku Ryoen looks more like an office building than a typical graveyard. The facility exudes a corporate feel, starting with the neatly dressed public relations woman who met us in the lobby. She worked for Nichiryoku Co., overall the third largest Japanese funeral company, but number one in the indoor cemeteries and graves market. "We are the pioneers of indoor facilities," she explained, "and the only large funeral company that is listed on the Tokyo Stock Exchange."

My DIY bias led me to identify more with the quirky-independent-monk light-up-Buddha team, but I had to admit that Nichiryoku Co. had discovered a market. In the 1980s, the price of land in Tokyo skyrocketed. In the 1990s a tiny grave could go for 6 million yen ($53,000 US). The market was ripe for more affordable, convenient, urban options (say, a cemetery right off the train).

Of course, being close to the train station isn't what makes the cemetery high-tech. The facility manager took us on a tour, starting with a long hallway with hyper-reflective black flooring and bright white overhead lighting. Lining each wall were individual pods, with privacy coverings made of translucent green glass. The whole impression was that of a 1980s movie imagining "the future," a design choice I endorsed.

Inside the pods, behind the glass, stood traditional granite gravestones. Each stone had a rectangular hole at the base, the size of a textbook. Fresh flowers sat in a vase, and incense waited to be lit. The manager took out a touch card similar to the one used at the Ruriden columbarium. Simulating what a family member would do, he touched the card to an electronic keypad. "The Sakura card recognizes the urn," he explained. Glass doors slid shut, hiding the gravestone.

Behind the scenes, magic was happening. I heard the dull whir of the robot's arm as it plucked our urn from among 4,700 others. After about a minute the glass doors opened to reveal the gravestone. The rectan-

gular hole now contained the urn, with a family symbol and name personalized on the front. "The idea is that many people can use the facility. We can store as many as possible," the manager explained. The facility can accommodate 7,200 urns, and it is already more than half full. "If you have your own grave, at your own family cemetery you have to change the flowers, light the incense. It's a lot of work. Here we do that all for you."

Of course, for the griever truly on the go, there is now an online service that allows for virtual grave visits. Another Tokyo company, I-Can Corp., presents a Sims-like experience in which your ancestor's virtual gravestone appears on screen in a green field. The user can, according to taste, light a virtual incense stick, place flowers, sprinkle water on the stone, and leave fruit and glasses of beer.

The president of I-Can Corp. acknowledged that "certainly, it is best to pay ancestors an actual visit." But, "our service is for those who believe that it is possible to pay their respects in front of a computer screen."

The head monk at Daitokuin Ryōgoku Ryoen, Masuda jūshoku, seemed permanently relaxed, and like Yajima jūshoku, had no problems with Buddhism mixing old and new ideas. (As we left he cycled away on his bike, in full robes, talking on his cellphone). The facility was a partner project between his temple and Nichiryoku Co. Years of planning went into the high-rise cemetery, which opened to the public in 2013.

"Well, you've seen the facility, what do you think of it?" he asked wryly.

"It's more technology-based than any cemetery we have in the United States," I replied. "And everything is so clean here, from the cemeteries to the cremation machines. Everything is cleaner, and much less industrial."

"Well, dealing with death has become cleaner," he acknowledged. "People used to fear the dead body, but we've made it clean. And then the cemeteries became like a park, neat and clean."

Masuda indulged me in a long conversation about cremation trends in both Japan and America. We discussed how the Japanese were moving away from the *kotsuage,* in which the family personally removes the bones, preferring instead to have the facility's employees grind the bones down and scatter them. "Traditionally, Japanese people are concerned with the skeleton," he explained. "They perform the *kotsuage,* as you know. They like the bones, they don't want ash."

"Then what has changed?" I asked.

"There are feelings that come with the bones, responsibility for the soul. Bones are real," Masuda said. "The people who scatter the ash are trying to forget. Trying to put aside the things they don't want to think about."

"Do you think that's a good thing?" I asked.

"I don't think it's a good thing. You can try to make death cleaner, but especially after the big earthquake, and with the suicide rate being very high, death has come closer. There are people who take their lives before the age of ten. People are beginning to think about death. You can't ignore it anymore."

There was a time when the Japanese feared the corpse as unclean and impure. They have largely overcome that fear and have begun to see the body in the casket not for what it was, but for *who* it belonged to — not a cursed object, but a beloved grandpa. The Japanese make an effort to integrate rituals with the body, and ensure the family has enough time to spend in its presence. Meanwhile, countries like the U.S. have done the reverse. Once we cared for our corpses at home. Before the rise of the professional death class we did not have the fear the Japanese had of the dead, and we valued the presence of the corpse. But in recent years we have been taught to see the dead as unclean and impure, and fear of the physical dead body has risen, along with our direct cremation rate.

What's more, and what sets them apart, is that the Japanese have not been afraid to integrate technology and innovation in their funerals and memorials. We don't have a single space like Ruriden with its glowing Buddhas or Daitokuin Ryōoku Ryoen with its robot retrieval system. Our funeral homes are considered high-tech if they offer online obituaries or a photo slideshow during the funeral.

If anything, the Japanese funeral market can prove to Western countries that you don't have to choose between technology and interaction with the dead body. Even better, you can offer *both* options to clients at your funeral home and not destroy your bottom line. And yes, more than ever, I want a corpse hotel.

BOLIVIA:
LA PAZ

Paul Koudounaris was wearing a large fuzzy hat made from a coyote pelt, with the ears still attached. The hat, worn in combination with the gold beads that hung from his pointy black beard, made him look like Genghis Khan on his way to a furry convention.

"I think Doña Ely will like the coyote hat," he explained. "She dresses her cat up like a Jedi." In Paul's mind, this was a perfectly reasonable connection.

Doña Ely lived three blocks behind the back wall of La Paz's General Cemetery, down a cobblestone street, in a nondescript home with a single threadbare sheet hanging in the doorway. Many residences on the street had similar features: corrugated roofs, wooden walls, concrete floors. But Doña Ely's was the only home that also had a rack of sixty-seven human skulls, wearing matching cotton beanies, ready to grant favors to their many fervent devotees.

The sixty-seven skulls in Doña Ely's house were *ñatitas*. The name translates to "flat noses" or "little pug-nosed ones," an adorable infantilization of a skull. To be a *ñatita* is to have special powers to connect the living and the dead. As Paul put it, *"Ñatitas* have to be human skulls, but not every skull gets to be a *ñatita."*

These skulls did not belong to Doña Ely's friends or family members. The skulls appeared to Doña Ely in dreams, alerting her to their presence. She went to collect them from overcrowded cemeteries, markets, archeological sites, and medical schools. Doña Ely acts as their special caretaker, making offerings to them in return for help with everything from diabetes to debt.

Doña Ely recognized Paul right away; he has been coming to La Paz to photograph *ñatitas* for the past eleven years. (And, to recap, Paul is pretty recognizable.)

"Dónde está su gato?" he asked. ("Where is your cat?")

Doña Ely and Paul share two cross-cultural connections: one, their obvious love of skulls, and two, dressing up their cats in costume. Paul pulled out his cellphone and began to show Ely pictures of his own cat, Baba, dressed as "Cat-urday Night Fever" with a handlebar mustache, a gold neck chain, and a permed wig, and "Florence Nighten-tail" with nurse uniform and stethoscope.

"Aaaaah!" Doña Ely exclaimed in delight, recognizing a true kindred spirit.

The skulls, on the other hand, wore identical cotton beanies, light blue in color, with their individual names embroidered on the front, like babies in a nursery: Ramiro, Carlota, Jose, Waldo (found him!). These weren't their names originally; the names were bestowed by Doña Ely when the skulls became *ñatitas*.

Each one of Doña Ely's *ñatitas* has a distinct personality, and a distinct gift. Carlitos is the skull you'd visit for medical issues; Cecilia helps students studying at university. Seven of the skulls, including Maria and Cielo, were the skulls of children and infants, so they specialize in children's issues. The skulls had coca leaves in their mouths, and the crevices between them were stuffed with brightly wrapped candy. Other offerings made to the *ñatitas* by their estimated two to three hundred devotees included flowers, bottles of soda, and entire watermelons and pineapples.

Certain skulls were considered the most powerful, the heavy hitters. Oscar sat on the top shelf wearing a police cap. Oscar was the first of Doña Ely's *ñatitas,* acquired eighteen years ago. "We had lost our house, had no work, no money," she explained, "and Oscar helped us to get back on our feet." Doña Ely can say with certainty that the *ñatitas* work miracles, because she has experienced the miracles for herself.

Another powerful *ñatita* was Sandra, and it was easy to see why. At least a quarter of Doña Ely's *ñatitas* were not as much skulls as they were mummified heads, and Sandra was the pièce de résistance. She had one of the more elegantly preserved heads I have ever seen, chubby-cheeked and smiling. Leathery skin covered the entirety of her face, including her lips, which seemed to curl up into a jovial smile. Two thick salt-and-pepper braids wound down the sides of her head. Even her nose was intact (rare, and hardly qualifying her as "pug-nosed"). In a feminist move, Sandra's specialty was financial negotiations and business.

Paul came closer to take photographs of Sandra. "Ah, here," Doña Ely said, sensing he was trying to get a tighter shot. She pulled Sandra from the shelf and removed her "Sandra" beanie, revealing the full extent of the preservation. Doña Ely looked around, searching for an even nicer acces-

sory for Sandra's close-up. As she went to fetch it, she handed Sandra's head to me.

"Oh, yeah, okay, sure," I fumbled.

When I held Sandra close, I could see her eyelids and a full set of light, fluttery eyelashes. If she had been acquired by a medical or history museum in the U.S., glass would have separated us. In La Paz, it was just me and — alas, poor Sandra.

Doña Ely returned with a tall white top hat for Sandra and plopped it on her head. Paul was snapping photos. "Okay, hold Sandra up closer to you, there we go," he said. "Caitlin, can you smile a little, you look so dour."

"This is a human head. I don't need

pictures of me grinning with a severed human head," I said.

"Sandra's smiling way more than you are, try to look a *little* less melancholy, please."

After I returned Sandra to the shelves and we prepared to leave, I noticed a brand-new set of teal embroidered beanies stacked next to the door. A woman waiting her turn to consult with Doña Ely's *ñatitas* explained, "Oh, they get a new color every month. Last month it was orange. These are the new ones. I like this color. It's going to look good on them."

Doña Ely has a significant collection of *ñatitas* ("I've photographed charnel houses with fewer skulls than Doña Ely's house," said Paul), but the most well-known *ñatitas* belong to Doña Ana. Full disclosure: I never actually saw Doña Ana. On the day we visited, a whole room of people were waiting around a huge cast-iron cauldron to enjoy an audience with her. Doña Ana's *ñatitas* speak to her in dreams, and based on your problem she will tell you which of the skulls to consult (Jose Maria, Nacho, Angel, Angel 2, and the very popular Jhonny).

Each of Doña Ana's two dozen *ñatitas* sat atop a glittering pillow in its own glass-fronted box. They wore safari hats with flowers along the brim. Cotton balls were stuffed in their eye sockets. Strips of tinfoil covered their upper and lower teeth, like metal mouthguards.

"What is the tinfoil for?" I asked Paul.

"To protect their teeth when they smoke," he said.

"They smoke?"

"Why wouldn't they?"

The Roman Catholic Church, as a general rule, has never thrilled to the presence of the *ñatitas* in La Paz. In the past, priests presiding over the annual Fiesta de las Ñatitas have announced to the crowds seeking blessings that the "skulls must be buried" and "should not be venerated."

The first year Paul came to photograph the Fiesta, people arrived to find the church at the General Cemetery locked, with a sign saying they would not be blessing any skulls. The people protested, marching through the streets, holding their *ñatitas* in the air and chanting, "We want blessings." The church opened its doors.

The Archbishop of La Paz, Edmundo Abastoflor, has been a particularly vocal dissenter on the subject of *ñatitas*. "Well, of course he has," Paul scoffed. "The *ñatitas* embarrass him. They make it look like he doesn't have control over his own diocese."

Women like Doña Ana and Doña Ely represent a threat to the Catholic Church. Through magic, belief, and their *ñatitas,* they facilitate a direct, unmediated connection to the powers of the beyond, no male intermediary required. It reminded me of Santa Muerte, the Mexican Saint of Death, who is unapologetically female. She carries a scythe and her long robes are vividly colored, draped over her skeletal form.

To the chagrin of the Church, Santa Muerte's devotees have spread to the southwestern United States, coming north from Mexico where she has tens of millions of followers. Her power is associated with outlaws, the poor, LGBT folk, criminals — anyone cast out from the stern bosom of Catholicism.

We cannot single out Catholicism as the only belief system with a history of dismissing the agency of female devotees. Regardless of a woman's more egalitarian place in modern Buddhism, the ancient scriptures tell of the Buddha encouraging his community of male monks to take trips to the charnel grounds to meditate on women's rotting bodies. The motive of these "meditations on foulness" was to liberate a monk from his desire for women; they were, as

231

scholar Liz Wilson calls them, "sensual stumbling blocks." The hope was that charnel meditation would strip women of all their desirable qualities so men would realize they are merely flesh-sacks filled with blood, guts, and phlegm. The Buddha was explicit, claiming that a woman's deception is not in her accessories, like makeup and gowns, but in her fraudulent garment of flesh, surreptitiously oozing grotesque liquids from its orifices.

Of course, these silent, decaying women of the charnel grounds were not permitted to have needs, desires, or spiritual journeys of their own to take. Wilson, again, explains that "in their role as teachers they do not utter a single word. What they have to teach is not what is on their minds but what is going on in their bodies." The charnel corpses are mere objects, delusion-busters for men to meditate on and thus gain the status of "worthy."

This was not the case at Doña Ana's, where women and their inner lives and problems were placed front and center. Nothing romantic, financial, or domestic was dismissed as a trivial issue. Her *ñatitas* were housed in a front room of her home, its walls covered from floor to ceiling in newspaper. Devotees had brought flowers and candles as offerings. Paul and I had brought white tapered candles, purchased from a roadside stall. I thought we would just hand over the candles as a gift, but one of Doña Ana's devotees insisted we light them as an offering. Squatting on the concrete floor, Paul and I burned each candle on the bottom, melting the wax to get them to stand vertical on metal plates. They kept falling over as we made a mess of this task, narrowly avoiding an inferno.

Since we had brought the offerings, I figured I had better talk to one of the *ñatitas*. I asked Nacho to influence the U.S. presidential election, which was being held the next day. I can only assume that either Nacho was not the right *ñatita* for American political matters or was rusty in his English.

A young woman sat among the *ñatitas*, with a small boy in her arms. "This is my first time here," she admitted. "A friend told me it would help with university, and to keep my boy safe, so here I am."

At dinner one night, Andres Bedoya, a friend of Paul's and an artist from La Paz, warned me that I "should not make the mistake of thinking we are a homogenous culture here in Bolivia." His latest works are burial shrouds, each taking five months to

233

create, handcrafted of leather, nails, and thousands of golden disks. "The artisans of Bolivia are sometimes looked down on, as if what they produce is not 'real' art. It is art, of course, and I let that inspire me."

Andres creates his shrouds for museums and galleries. In creating this "clothing for ghosts" he ritualizes his own grief, and the grief of others. He wouldn't be opposed to actually burying someone in the shrouds, but has yet to do so. Bolivians may not be homogenous, but funeral customs around La Paz tend to follow prescribed patterns. A solemn, daylong wake is held in the home or funeral parlor. Families hire a local service to deliver a coffin, along with crosses and flowers that light up and glow neon purple (the Bolivian color of death). "Some people think the glowing purple is tacky or

kitschy, but I love it," Andres admitted. Burial happens the next day. The coffin is carried for a block behind the hearse before being loaded in and driven to the cemetery.

Andres's mother died twenty-two years ago, and it was her wish to be cremated. Cremation in La Paz is growing in popularity, but until recently it was challenging to effectively cremate bodies there. At 12,000 feet, La Paz is the highest-altitude capital city in the world. The ovens "couldn't get hot enough, there wasn't enough oxygen," Andres explained. Today's machines achieve higher temperatures and thus can fully cremate a body.

Now that the technology is available, Andres considered exhuming his mother's body to honor her desire to be cremated. Unfortunately, the cemetery would require

that he come to identify her exhumed body in person. "Sure, I remember what she was wearing when we buried her, but I'd prefer not to have the memory of her bones. I don't need to carry that with me," he said.

It was his interest in death that led Andres to explore the culture of the *ñatitas*. November 8 is the Fiesta de las Ñatitas, a chance for the owners of the *ñatitas* to bring out the skulls and display them. The party is not for the owners, but for the skulls themselves, making sure the *ñatitas* are esteemed and validated for the work they've done throughout the year. "One tends to be very romantic and say the whole festival should remain untouched. But if it were completely untouched, you or I wouldn't be anywhere near it," Andres said.

Though unknown in most of the world, "the festival has almost entered the pop culture realm here," he explained. The General Cemetery, where the Fiesta de las Ñatitas is held, was once the cemetery for the wealthy, but they have moved south. The city has made recent attempts at revitalizing the cemetery, commissioning murals by street artists on the sides of mausoleums and encouraging local tourism. On All Saints Day live theater is performed at night, and thousands of locals show up.

The persistence of *ñatitas* in La Paz is due to the Aymara people, the second largest of Bolivia's indigenous groups. Discrimination against the Aymara was rampant for years. Until the late twentieth century, it was assumed that urban Aymaran women, known as *cholitas,* would be denied entry into certain government offices, restaurants, and buses. "I'll just say it, Bolivia is not a safe country for women, period," Andres said. "We're the poorest country in South America. We have a special word, *feminicidio,* that means a homicide where a woman is targeted and killed for being a woman, usually by a partner."

There has been tangible improvement over the last ten years. Bolivia's president, Evo Morales, is Aymaran, and equality for Bolivia's many ethnicities was an important part of his platform. *Cholitas* are now reclaiming their identity, including their fashion — many-layered skirts, shawls, and tall bowler hats balanced precariously on their heads. They are also entering public life, not as servants but as journalists and government workers. At the end of Fiesta de las Ñatitas, when the cemetery closes its gates, the *cholitas* perform folkloric dances through the streets on their way to different parties. "Last year, their outfits, so tied to this notion of subservience, were printed with military camouflage. The men were *pissed*," laughed Andres, who photographed the dancers. "Folklore is not just historical in La Paz. It's contemporary. It's constantly innovating."

Despite the increasing acceptance of the Aymara and the *ñatitas,* when Bolivians are asked if they keep a *ñatita* at home or believe in their powers, many will still say, "Oh, no no no, they frighten me!" They don't wish to appear to be bad Catholics. There is still an underground aspect to the practice. Many more Bolivians (even the professional class, like chiropractors and bankers) keep *ñatitas* than would ever admit to it publicly.

"The owners are practicing Catholics, though," Paul interjected. "I have never photographed a house with a *ñatita* that didn't have a picture of Jesus or the Virgin Mary on the wall."

"That's part of why Bolivia is so weird, frankly," Andres said. "I was discussing with a friend recently about how we are not a 'blend' of Catholicism and indigenous beliefs — they just got stuck together." He put the backs of his hands together, creating an awkward, monstrous shape. "My sister's office still has a *yatiri* [healer or witch doctor] who comes in to cleanse the space.

My father was a geologist, and when I was young I used to visit the mines with him. On one of those trips I witnessed the sacrifice of a llama, because the miners demanded it. They wanted to keep El Tío, ruler of the underworld, happy. These strains of magic are still everywhere."

The morning of November 8, Ximena set her Disney tote bag, which depicted Mickey Mouse and Donald Duck playing soccer, on the concrete entryway outside the church at the General Cemetery. One by one she pulled out her four *ñatitas,* setting them up on a wooden plank. I asked her to introduce them to me. Her oldest skull had belonged to Lucas, her uncle. I mentioned that the skulls are usually from strangers, but sometimes they can be members of the person's family. "He protects my house from robbery," she explained.

Each of Ximena's *ñatitas* had its own woven beanie, crowned by a wreath of flowers. She has brought them to the Fiesta de las Ñatitas for many years. "Do you bring them to thank them?" I asked.

"Well, to thank them, yes, but really this is their day. It's their celebration," she corrected me.

In the middle of our conversation, the

front door of the church opened and the crowd rushed through with skulls in tow, jockeying to get as close to the altar as possible. The newer attendees held back, tentatively waiting in the pews, but the experienced older women pushed their way forward and helped their friends send their skulls crowd-surfing up to the front.

To the left of the altar, a life-sized Jesus sculpture lay in a glass box. He was bleeding copiously from his forehead and cheeks. His bloody feet protruded from underneath a purple sheet. A woman carrying a *ñatita* in a cardboard chocolate wafer box stopped at his heels and crossed herself, then pushed

through the crowd toward the altar.

Despite the contentious relationship with the Catholic Church, the priest standing in front of the crowd today struck a surprisingly conciliatory tone. "When you have faith," he said, "you don't have to answer to anyone. Each of us has a different story. This is a birthday celebration, in a way. I am happy we are all together, this is a small piece of happiness."

A young woman, crammed next to me in the crowd, explained the priest's acceptance of the skulls this way: "This festival is so big now, even the Catholic Church had to bend."

The skulls and their owners filed out from the two side doors of the church. At each door was a painter's bucket filled with holy water. Plastic roses served as aspergilla, sprinkling holy water onto the *ñatitas* as they passed. Some *ñatitas* wore sunglasses, others crowns. Some *ñatitas* had elaborate altars built just for them; others came in cardboard boxes. One woman had a baby *ñatita* in a fabric lunchbox cooler. The *ñatitas* got their blessing.

Bolivia is not the only place where skulls have connected believers to the divine. The irony behind the Church's disdain for the practice is that European Catholics have used saintly relics and bones as intermediaries for more than a thousand years. The *ñatitas* were similar in purpose to other skulls I had met several years earlier, on a trip to Naples, Italy.

"You are English?" my Neapolitan taxi driver asked.

"Close."

"Dutch?"

"American."

"Ah, Americana! Where am I taking you?"

"The Cimitero delle Fontanelle . . ." Here I consulted my crumpled itinerary. "In Materdei, via Fontanelle."

In the rearview mirror, I saw my taxi driver's eyebrows shoot up.

"Catacombs? The cemetery? No no no, you don't want to go there," he insisted.

"I don't?" I asked. "Are they not open today?"

"You are a pretty young lady. You are on holiday, no? You don't want to go to the catacombs; that's not for you. I'll take you to the beach. Napoli has many beautiful beaches. Which beach I take you to?"

"I'm not really the beach type," I explained.

"You are the catacomb type?" he shot back.

Now that he mentioned it, I was. That is, if the catacomb type could be anyone other than a dead person.

"Thanks, man, but let's stick with the Fontanelle Cemetery."

He shrugged his shoulders and off we sped through the winding, cobbled hills of Naples.

To call Fontanelle a cemetery is deceptive, as it is really more of a large white cave — a tuff quarry, to be exact. (Tuff is rock formed from volcanic ash.) For centuries, this tuff cave was used to bury Naples's poor and anonymous dead, from the seventeenth-century victims of the plague to the cholera deaths of the mid-1800s.

By 1872, Father Gaetano Barbati made it his mission to arrange, stack, sort, and catalogue the bones stuffed into the Fontanelle Cemetery. Volunteers from the city came to help, and, like good Catholics, prayed for the anonymous dead as they piled skulls along one wall, femurs along another. The problem was, the skull prayers did not stop there.

Spontaneously, a cult of devotion sprung up around the unnamed skulls. Locals would come to Fontanelle to visit their *pezzentelle,* or "poor little ones." They would "adopt" certain skulls, cleaning them, building them shrines, bringing them offerings, and asking for favors. The skulls were given new names, revealed to their owners in dreams.

The Catholic Church was not pleased. They even closed the cemetery in 1969, with the Archbishop of Naples decreeing that the Cult of the Dead was "arbitrary" and "superstitious." According to the Church, you could pray for souls trapped in Purgatory (like these anonymous dead), but the anonymous dead had no special, supernatural powers to grant the living favors. The living begged to differ.

Scholar Elizabeth Harper pointed out that the Cult of the Dead was strongest and "most noticeable during times of strife: specifically among women affected by disease, natural disaster, or war." The most important factor was that these women "lack access to power and resources within the Catholic Church." (This idea was echoed by Andres Bedoya, the artist 6,500 miles away in La Paz, who described the *ñatitas* as potent to those women "whose connection with the beyond wasn't being properly managed by the Catholic Church.")

Vigilant though the Church may have been since reopening the Fontanelle Cemetery in 2010, the Cult of the Dead has not disappeared. Amidst a sea of white bone, dashes of color burst out. Neon plastic rosaries, red glass candles, fresh gold coins, prayer cards, plastic Jesuses, and even lottery tickets are scattered throughout the ruins. A new generation of the Cult of the Dead has found their most powerful *pezzentelle.*

By 11 a.m. the Fiesta de las Ñatitas was packed. The rows of graves were lined with blessed *ñatitas,* now accepting offerings of coca leaves and flower petals. Police patrolled the cemetery's entrance gates, checking bags for alcohol (booze-related violence has led to the creation of new *ñatitas*). In the absence of alcohol, the skulls had to indulge in other vices. Lit cigarettes burned down to tar-stained teeth.

"Do you suppose they enjoy the smoking?" I asked Paul.

"Well, obviously they enjoy it," he said dismissively, before disappearing into the crowd, wearing his coyote hat.

One woman danced with her *ñatita* to the raucous sounds of a live accordion, guitar, and wooden drum, thrusting this skull into the air and shaking her hips. This was the skull's day, his celebration.

A man sat with the skull of his father. At one point his father had been buried right here in the General Cemetery. This forced me to wonder: if his father had been interred, how had his son gotten the skull back, the skull who now wore wire-rim eyeglasses and seven flower crowns piled high on his head?

When I walked through the cemetery there were empty graves surrounded by smashed glass and hunks of concrete. Attached to the front of the tombs were yellowed pieces of paper with notices that read some version of "FINAL WARNING: Mausoleum, 4th of January. To the relatives of the late: (Insert name here) . . ."

What followed was a message stating that the families had not paid the rental fees for keeping Dad's body in the mausoleum. As a result, he was getting evicted. Perhaps he would go into a communal grave. Or perhaps he would return to his family, now skeletonized, to become a *ñatita*.

As I crouched, examining a mummified *ñatita,* with its lip curled up in a distinct Elvis Presley sneer, a woman my age sidled up to me. In near-perfect English she said, "So, you're from the other side of the pond, you must be like, 'What the fuck is this?' "

Her name was Moira, and she came every

year to the Fiesta with her friend, who kept two *ñatitas* in his home. His first *ñatita,* the most powerful, came to him in a dream. In the dream she informed him she would be waiting for him in the countryside. He went and found her, and named her Diony. Then came Juanito. People come to his home all year round to visit them.

"My sister lost her cat," Moira said. "She's single, so this cat is like her baby. For four days the cat doesn't come back."

Her sister went to consult Diony the *ñatita,* asking for help finding the beloved feline. In a dream, Diony revealed that the cat was in the back of an abandoned car, with plants growing inside.

"Up the hill behind where my sister lives, there is a hollowed-out car that has been there for fifteen years. And there's the stupid cat, trapped in a hole in the back of the car!

"This was a week ago," Moira explained, "and to be safe, my sister also asked Diony to scare the cat, to make sure it wouldn't run away again. Now it won't even go beyond the border of the yard, like it's being yanked back by a leash."

I wondered if Moira believed that the power of the skull had really found this cat. She thought for a moment. "It's the faith people have when they ask. That's what matters."

Moira thought longer and then added, grinning, "I can't tell you if it was a co-incidence or not. Either way, we found the cat!"

Any answered prayer can be viewed as a coincidence or not. I wasn't in La Paz to determine whether the *ñatitas* had true magical powers. I was more interested in women like Doña Ely and Doña Ana, and the hundreds of other people at the Fiesta, who were using their comfort with death to seize direct access to the divine from the hands of the male leaders of the Catholic Church. As Paul bluntly put it, the skulls are "technology for disadvantaged people." No problem — whether love, family, or school — is too small for a *ñatita,* and no person is left behind.

CALIFORNIA: JOSHUA TREE

Sometimes you visit corpses all around the world and realize that the corpses dearest to your heart are right in your own backyard. When I returned to Los Angeles, my funeral home awaited — along with my long-suffering funeral director, Amber, who facilitated cremations and comforted distraught families while I was off requesting help with mutual funds from a Bolivian skull.

Undertaking LA had an un-embalmed, natural burial scheduled for Mrs. Shepard. Inspired by what I had seen on my travels, I returned to work with a new sense of purpose. In my mind, the grieving family would prepare the body with love, wrapping the dead woman in a handmade shroud lined with peacock feathers and palm fronds. We'd lead a procession to the grave at dawn, carrying candles and scattering flower petals, chanting as we went.

This burial — well — wasn't like that.

By the time we got Mrs. Shepard into our body preparation room, she had been dead for six weeks, trapped in a plastic body bag under refrigeration at the L.A. coroner's office. Amber and I stood on either side of her as we unzipped her bag. Mold had begun to grow under her eyes, and carried down her neck and onto her shoulders. Her stomach was collapsed, colored deep aquamarine (brought on by the decomposition of the red blood cells). The top layers of skin peeled free from her calves. The bag had been swamplike, bathing Mrs. Shepard in her own blood and bodily fluid.

We released her from the plastic prison and washed her body down, soapy water sliding down the steel table and disappearing through a small hole near her feet. Amber washed her hair, originally white but now dyed brown with blood, doing her best to work around the patches of mold growing on her scalp. We labored in silence, something about the decayed state of the body making us less vocal than usual. After patting Mrs. Shepard dry, it was clear that she was not done leaking. If Undertaking LA were a typical mortuary, we'd have all types of tricks up our sleeves (Saran Wrap, diapers, chemical powders, even head-to-

toe plastic body suits) to combat the aptly named "leakage." But a natural cemetery won't accept a body for burial that has been treated with any of those chemical leakage treatments.

We moved Mrs. Shepard straight into her shroud, hoping to wrap her enough times that she wouldn't ooze through. Amber had sewn the shroud herself from unbleached cotton fabric. The family had little money, and we were trying to bring down costs everywhere we could. The day before, I had received a text from Amber: a picture of a receipt from JoAnn's Fabrics with the caption, "Guess who just saved the family 40% on their burial shroud with JoAnn's points!" The finished product was charming, complete with ties and handles (though no peacock feathers or palm fronds).

A shrouded Mrs. Shepard was placed into the back of a van and driven two and a half hours east of Los Angeles, through the Inland Empire (a deceptive Tolkien-like name for what is essentially clusters of suburbs) and finally into the Mojave Desert. You know you've reached desert not from the change of landscape but from the casino billboards, advertising performances from a rotating cast of slightly less relevant celebrities. (This particular drive: Michael Bolton and Ludacris.) Then you are well and truly in the desert, among the Joshua trees, *Yucca brevifolia,* with their spiky arms reaching to the sky in whimsical, Seussian poses.

Joshua Tree Memorial Park was not created to be a natural cemetery. They have done what many cemeteries (of sense) are doing, and dedicated a section of their land to offer natural burials. The distance to Joshua Tree is often prohibitive for a Los Angeles family. We Angelenos would prefer to keep our dead closer to home, but where? Forest Lawn Memorial Park, one of L.A.'s celebrity burial spots, insists on heavy vaults surrounding the caskets, and doesn't offer natural burial. They do make exceptions for Jews and Muslims, both religions that require the natural burial of bodies. In these cases, they agree to poke holes in the concrete of the vault for symbolic dirt to trickle through.

A natural section has recently opened at Woodlawn Cemetery in Santa Monica. But to purchase a plot there you'll pay a several-thousand-dollar "green" premium, even though a natural burial is easier to accomplish (if you need to go scream into a pillow in frustration, I'll wait).

Joshua Tree's natural burial section

opened in 2010. They set aside sixty burial plots, forty of which are now filled, in a plot of land surrounded by a low wooden fence. The natural burial section, tiny compared to the vast desert surrounding it, further highlights how ludicrous our modern policies on burial are. The world used to be our burial ground. We buried bodies on farms, ranches, and in local churchyards — anywhere we wanted, really. Some states still allow for burial on private property. But California is not one of them, and our corpses must be herded into small pens in the desert.

One of the priests I met in Japan, Masuda

jūshoku, had heard that the cremation rate in America was rising in part because of fears we might run out of land in which to bury people. He didn't understand this motivation. "From my Japanese perspective, the U.S. is a big country. There is *so* much land everywhere, it would be very easy to build these big cemeteries and graves."

Some picture a "green" burial and need that directive to be literal: verdant rolling hills, dense forests, burial under a willow tree. Joshua Tree, with its stocky cholla pencil cacti, creosote bushes, and globemallows fighting their way through the sandy soil, can seem a harsh landscape, not a place of mystical regeneration.

But the desert has always nurtured the rebels, the wild-hearted. Alt-country musician Gram Parsons was only twenty-six when he overdosed on a combo of heroin, morphine, and alcohol in his hotel room in Joshua Tree. His (underlined: allegedly) wicked step-father wanted Parsons's body flown back to New Orleans so he could take control of his estate, in the erroneous belief that to the body-holder go the spoils.

Parsons's good friend Phil Kaufman had other plans. The two men had made a pact that if one of them died, "the survivor would take the other guy's body out to Joshua

Tree, have a few drinks and burn it."

Somehow, through charm and brazen drunkenness, Kaufman and an accomplice managed to track down Parsons's casket at Los Angeles International Airport and prevent it from being loaded onto the plane to New Orleans by convincing an airline employee that the Parsons family had changed their minds. The duo even got a police officer and an airline employee to help them transfer Parsons's body into a makeshift hearse (no license plate, broken windows, filled with liquor). Off they drove, Parsons rattling in the back.

When they reached Cap Rock, a natural boulder formation in Joshua Tree National Park, they removed the casket, doused Parsons's body with fuel, and set it on fire, sending a colossal fireball shooting into the night sky.

The two men fled. A coating of fuel is not enough to fully cremate a body, and Parsons was recovered as a semi-charred corpse. For all their antics, Kaufman and his accomplice were charged only with misdemeanor theft for stealing the casket (not the body, mind you). What was left of Parsons's body was sent to New Orleans, where it was buried. His stepfather never got the money.

Mrs. Shepard, for her part, did not have a

"throw back a few drinks and burn it" advance directive for her mortal remains. She had, however, been a liberal activist and environmental advocate her whole life, and her family felt that embalming and a metal casket would be against everything she stood for.

Tony, a Joshua Tree native covered in tattoos, had dug the four-foot grave by hand early in the morning, before the unforgiving sun rose. A pile of sandy, decomposed granite soil was piled next to the grave, and four plain wooden boards spanned the hole.

We hand-carried Mrs. Shepard to the site and laid her shrouded corpse on the boards, where it hovered above the grave below. In her shroud, you could see the outline of her body. It was Grade A humility, just as burial would have been when this land was still wild — the only elements being a shovel, some wood, a shroud, and a dead man or woman. Three cemetery employees pulled Mrs. Shepard a few inches off the boards with long straps, as I knelt down and slid the boards out from beneath her. Then they lowered her while Tony the gravedigger hopped in beside her to see her safely to the dirt below.

After a moment of silence, the three men, working with shovels and rakes, brought the

soil down, on top of Mrs. Shepard. Halfway
through the process they placed a heavy
layer of stone, to deter interested coyotes
(this step appears to be mostly superstitious,
as there is no evidence that natural cemeteries attract the notice of scavenger animals).
Filling the grave took all of ten minutes. In
other cemeteries, the burial process disturbs
the grass, leaving the stark, obvious outline
of a grave amid the symmetrical green
landscape. When Tony and his crew had
finished you couldn't tell where the grave
was. Mrs. Shepard had disappeared into the
endless desert.

That is what I want in death: to disappear. If I'm lucky, I will disappear, swallowed by the ground like Mrs. Shepard. But that wouldn't be my first choice.

In two minutes they re-appeared with the empty bier and white cloth; and scarcely had they closed the door when a dozen vultures swooped down upon the body, and were rapidly followed by others. In five minutes more we saw the satiated birds fly back and lazily settle down again upon the parapet. They had left nothing behind but a skeleton.

In 1876, *The Times* of London described that scene at a *dakhma,* known in the West by its ominous translation, tower of silence. That day, swarms of vultures devoured a human body down to its skeleton in minutes. This consumption is exactly what the Parsis (descendants of the Iranian followers of Zoroastrianism) desire for their corpses. The religion regards the elements — earth, fire, water — as sacred, not to be defiled by an unclean dead body. Cremation and burial are off-limits as disposal options.

The Parsis built their first towers of

silence in the late thirteenth century. Today there are three towers that sit high on a hill in an exclusive, wealthy neighborhood in Mumbai. A circular brick amphitheater with an open ceiling, a tower of silence features concentric circles on which are placed the eight hundred dead bodies brought to the towers every year. The outer circle is for men, the middle circle for women, the innermost circle for children. In the center, the bones (post-vulture) are collected, to slowly decompose into the soil.

A Parsi funeral is an elaborate ritual. The body is covered in cow's urine and washed by the family and attendants from the tower. There are recitations, a sacred burning fire, continuous vigils, and prayers throughout the night. Only then is the body brought into the tower.

This ancient ritual has hit a roadblock in recent years. There was a time when India had a vulture population of 400 million. In 1876, the swift devouring of the body was the norm. "Parsis speak of a time when vultures would be waiting for bodies at the towers of silence," explained Harvard lecturer on Zoroastrianism Yuhan Vevaina. "Today, there are none."

It is hard to cremate without fire. It is even harder to dispose of a body via vulture

without vultures. The vulture population has dropped 99 percent. In the early 1990s, India allowed the use of diclofenac (a mild painkiller similar to ibuprofen) for ailing cattle. Hoof and udder pain were eased, but when the animal perished and the faithful vultures soared down for the meal, the diclofenac caused their kidneys to fail. It seems unfair that such iron-stomached creatures, used to devouring rotting carrion in the hot sun, could be felled by something akin to Advil.

Without the vultures, the bodies in the towers of silence lie waiting for the sky-dancers who will never show. The neighbors can smell them. Dhan Baria's mother was placed in the tower when she died in 2005. One of the tower attendants told Baria that the bodies lie exposed and half rotten, with not a vulture in sight. She hired a photographer to sneak in, and the resulting photographs (showing bodies indeed lying exposed and half rotten) caused a scandal in the Parsi community.

The tower attendants tried to get around the lack of vultures. They set up mirrors to concentrate solar energy on a group of corpses, like a nine-year-old zapping bugs with a magnifying glass. But the solar blasting doesn't work during the cloudy monsoon season. They tried pouring dissolving chemicals straight into the bodies, but that made an unpleasant mess. Family members like Dhan Baria ask why Parsis cannot shift and adapt their traditions, try burial or cremation so that bodies like her mother's are not left intact on cold stone. But the priests are obstinate. Vultures or no, there will be no change to the towers of silence.

This is the ultimate irony. There are people in the United States enamored with the thought of giving their bodies to animals at the end of their lives — and we have more than enough vultures and other scavenger animals to pull it off. But the government, religious leaders, etc., would never allow such a vile spectacle on American soil. No, our leaders tell us: cremation and burial, those are your options.

Dhan Baria, and a growing number of Parsis disturbed at the treatment of their dead, would like to explore cremation or burial. No, their leaders tell them: vultures, that is your option.

Since I first discovered sky burial I have known what I wanted for my mortal remains. In my view burial by animals is the safest, cleanest, and most humane way of disposing of corpses, and offers a new ritual that might bring us closer to the realities of death and our true place on this planet.

In the mountains of Tibet, where wood for cremation is scarce and the ground too rocky and frozen for burial, they have practiced celestial burial for thousands of years.

A dead man is wrapped in cloth in the fetal position, the position he was born from. Buddhist lamas chant over the body before it is handed over to the *rogyapa,* the body breaker. The *rogyapa* unwraps the body and slices into the flesh, sawing away the skin and strips of muscle and tendon. He sharpens his machete on nearby rocks. In his white apron, he resembles a butcher, the corpse appearing more animal than human.

263

Of all the death professionals in the world, *rogyapa* is the job I do not envy. A *rogyapa* interviewed by the BBC said, "I have performed many sky burials. But I still need some whiskey to do it."

Nearby, the vultures have already begun to gather. They are Himalayan griffon vultures, bigger than you'd imagine, with nine-foot wingspans. The vultures tighten ranks, emitting guttural screeches as men hold them back with long rods. They huddle in groupings so tight that they become a giant ball of feathers.

The *rogyapa* pounds the defleshed bones with a mallet, crushing them together with *tsama,* barley flour mixed with yak butter or milk. The *rogyapa* may strategically lay the bones and cartilage out first, and hold back the best pieces of flesh. He doesn't want the vultures to have their fill of the best cuts of meat and lose interest, flying off before the entirety of the body is consumed.

The signal is given, the rods are retracted, and the vultures descend with violence. They shriek like beasts as they consume the carrion, but they are, at the same time, glorious sky-dancers, soaring upward and taking the body for its burial in the sky. It is a virtuous gift to give your body this way — returning the body back to nature, where it can be of use.

The citizens of the developed world are hopelessly drawn to this visceral, bloody disposition. Tibet struggles with what this increased thanotourism (*thano* being the Greek prefix for "death") means for their rituals. In 2005 the government issued a rule that banned sightseeing, photography, and video recording at the sky burial sites. But tour guides have still flooded the area, bringing four-wheel-drive vehicles full of tourists from eastern China. Even though the dead person's family is not present for the vulture portion of the ritual, two dozen Chinese tourists will be, iPhones poised at the ready. They aim to capture death without the tidy edges, like the boxed urns of cremated remains given to them back home.

There is a story of a Western tourist trying to get around the no-photography rule by hiding behind a rock and using a long-range telephoto lens, not realizing that his presence scared off the vultures who usually waited on that ridge. After being frightened off, they didn't show up to consume the corpse, which was considered a bad omen for the ritual.

I spent the first thirty years of my life devouring animals. So why, when I die, should they not have their turn with me?

Am I not an animal?

Tibet is the one place I wanted to go on my travels, but could not bring myself to do it. It is difficult to accept that, barring true societal change, I will never have this option for my corpse. What's more, I may never even witness this ritual in my lifetime. If I were the Westerner with the telephoto lens who scared off the vultures, I'd have to leave myself out for the birds as well.

EPILOGUE

On a crisp fall day in Vienna, Austria, I received a private tour of the crypt below Michaelerkirche (St. Michael's Church). Bernard, the young Austrian man who led me down the steep stone staircase, had perfect English delivered in an inexplicably deep Southern accent.

"Aye've been told my ax-sent is straynge be-fore," he drawled, like a Confederate general.

Bernard explained that during the Middle Ages, when the members of the Hapsburg court attended St. Michael's, there was a cemetery located directly outside, in the courtyard. But, as so often happened in larger European cities, the cemetery became overcrowded, "lay-urd with de-caying bodies" — so overcrowded, in fact, that the neighbors (that is to say, the Emperor) complained of the stench. The cemetery was closed and a crypt constructed deep beneath

St. Michael's in the seventeenth century.

Many of the thousands of bodies buried in the crypt were laid to rest on beds of woodchips inside wooden coffins. The woodchips soaked up the fluids from decomposition. The dryness that followed this fluid absorption, in combination with drafts of cool air flowing through the crypt, caused a spontaneous natural mummification of the bodies.

Bernard shone a flashlight onto a man's body, holding the beam on the spot where the lace bottom of his baroque-era wig clung to his taut grey skin. Down the row, past the typical stacks of bones and skulls found in charnel houses, the body of a woman was so well preserved that her nose still protruded outward from her face, some three hundred years after her death. Her delicate, articulated fingers lay crossed over her chest.

The church currently makes four of these crypt mummies available for public viewing. The questions visitors pose to Bernard should be obvious: "How did this mummification occur?" Or, "How did the church manage to beat the recent invasion of wooden coffin–devouring beetles from New Zealand?" (Answer: by installing air conditioning).

But what visitors, especially young visitors, really want to know is, "Are the bodies real?"

The question is posed as if the stacked bones and skulls, the rows of coffins, the rare mummies, could all be part of a spooky haunted-crypt attraction instead of the very history of the city in which they live.

At almost any location in any major city on Earth, you are likely standing on thousands of bodies. These bodies represent a history that exists, often unknown, beneath our feet. While a new Crossrail station was being dug in London in 2015, 3,500 bodies were excavated from a sixteenth- and seventeenth-century cemetery under Liverpool Street, including a burial pit from the Great Plague of 1665. To cremate bodies we burn fossil fuel, thus named because it is made of decomposed dead organisms. Plants grow from the decayed matter of former plants. The pages of this book are made from the pulp of raw wood from a tree felled in its prime. All that surrounds us comes from death, every part of every city, and every part of every person.

That autumn day in Vienna, my private tour of the crypt wasn't private because I possess an exclusive all-access corpse card. The tour was private because I was the only person who showed up.

Outside, in the courtyard that was once an overcrowded cemetery, groups of school-children swarmed. They waited impatiently to be herded into the Hofburg Palace to confront the relics of the past, jewels and golden scepters and cloaks. In the church just across the courtyard, down some steep stone steps, there were bodies that could teach the children more than any scepter. Hard evidence that all who came before them have died. All will die someday. We avoid the death that surrounds us at our own peril.

Death avoidance is not an individual fail-ing; it's a cultural one. Facing death is not for the faint-hearted. It is far too challeng-ing to expect that each citizen will do so on his or her own. Death acceptance is the responsibility of all death professionals — funeral directors, cemetery managers, hospital workers. It is the responsibility of those who have been tasked with creating physical and emotional environments where safe, open interaction with death and dead bodies is possible.

Nine years ago, when I began working with the dead, I heard other practitioners speak about holding the space for the dying person and their family. With my secular bias, "holding the space" sounded like saccharine hippie lingo.

This judgment was wrong. Holding the space is crucial, and exactly what we are missing. To hold the space is to create a ring of safety around the family and friends of the dead, providing a place where they can grieve openly and honestly, without fear of being judged.

Everywhere I traveled I saw this death space in action, and I felt what it means to be held. At Ruriden columbarium in Japan, I was held by a sphere of Buddhas glowing soft blue and purple. At the cemetery in Mexico, I was held by a single wrought-iron fence in the light of tens of thousands of flickering amber candles. At the open-air pyre in Colorado, I was held within the elegant bamboo walls, which kept mourners safe as the flames shot high. There was magic to each of these places. There was grief, unimaginable grief. But in that grief there was no shame. These were places to meet despair face to face and say, "I see you waiting there. And I feel you, strongly. But you do not demean me."

In our Western culture, where are we held in our grief? Perhaps religious spaces, churches, temples — for those who have faith. But for everyone else, the most vulnerable time in our lives is a gauntlet of awkward obstacles.

First come our hospitals, which are often perceived as cold, antiseptic horror shows. At a recent meeting, a longtime acquaintance of mine apologized for having been so hard to reach, but her mother had just died in a Los Angeles hospital. There had been an extended illness, and her mother spent her final weeks lying on a special inflatable mattress, designed to prevent the bedsores that can develop from long periods of immobility. After her death, the sympathetic nurses told my acquaintance that she could take the time she needed to sit with her mother's body. After a few minutes, a doctor strode into the room. The family had never met this doctor before, and he did not choose to introduce himself. He walked over to her mother's chart, read it briefly, and then leaned down and pulled the plug on the inflatable mattress. Her mother's life-less body sprang upward, jolting from side to side "like a zombie" as the air left the mattress. The doctor walked out, having not said a word. The family was far from held. As soon as their mother took her last breath, they were spat out.

Second, there are our funeral homes. An executive of Service Corporation International, the country's largest funeral and cemetery company, admitted recently that "the industry was really built around selling a casket." As fewer and fewer of us see value in placing Mom's made-up body in a $7,000 casket and turn to simple cremations instead, the industry must find a new way to survive financially, by selling not a "funeral service" but a "gathering" in a "multisensory experience room."

As a recent *Wall Street Journal* article explained: "Using audio and video equipment, the experience rooms can create the atmosphere of a golf course, complete with the scent of newly mowed grass, to salute the life of a golfing fanatic. Or it can conjure up a beach, mountain or football stadium."

Perhaps paying several thousand dollars to hold a funeral in a faux "multisensory" golf course will make families feel held in their grief, but I have my doubts.

My mother recently turned seventy. One afternoon, as an exercise, I envisioned taking my mother's mummified body out of the grave, as they do in Tana Toraja in Indonesia. Pulling her remains toward me, standing her up, looking her in the eyes years after her death — the thought no longer alarmed me. Not only could I handle such a task, I believe I would find solace in the ritual.

Holding the space doesn't mean swaddling the family immobile in their grief. It also means giving them meaningful tasks. Using chopsticks to methodically clutch bone after bone and place them in an urn, building an altar to invite a spirit to visit once a year, even taking a body from the grave to clean and redress it: these activities give the mourner a sense of purpose. A sense of purpose helps the mourner grieve. Grieving helps the mourner begin to heal.

We won't get our ritual back if we don't show up. Show up first, and the ritual will come. Insist on going to the cremation, insist on going to the burial. Insist on being involved, even if it is just brushing your mother's hair as she lies in her casket. Insist on applying her favorite shade of lipstick, the one she wouldn't dream of going to the grave without. Insist on cutting a small lock of her hair to place in a locket or a ring. Do not be afraid. These are human acts, acts of bravery and love in the face of death and loss.

I would be comfortable with my mother's dead body precisely because *I would be held.* The ritual doesn't involve sneaking into a cemetery in the dead of night to peek in on a mummy. The ritual involves pulling someone I loved, and thus my grief, out into the light of day. Greeting my mother, alongside my neighbors and family — my community standing next to me in support. Sunlight is the best disinfectant, they say. No matter what it takes, the hard work begins for the West to haul our fear, shame, and grief surrounding death out into the disinfecting light of the sun.

ACKNOWLEDGMENTS

Trust me, I didn't drag myself around the world without some *serious* help.

This book was darkness on the face of the deep. It was given form in the void by mother-agent Anna Sproul-Latimer and father-editor Tom Mayer. "Let there be book!" they said. And there was book.

All the other incredible folk on Team Caitlin at W. W. Norton, with special thanks to Steve Colca, Erin Sinesky Lovett, Sarah Bolling, Allegra Huston, Elizabeth Kerr, and Mary Kate Skehan.

The savage eyes who ripped apart early drafts of this book: Will C. White, Louise Hung, David Forrest, Mara Zehler, Will Slocombe, and Alex Frankel.

Paul Koudounaris . . . just for being you.

Sarah Chavez, for being my right-hand woman in all things and trusting me with your story.

My poor funeral director Amber Carvaly,

left to raise the funeral home by herself while I was an absentee owner.

Bianca Daalder-van Iersel and Conner Habib, for tossing me over the finish line kicking and screaming.

On my travels: all the inspiring members of the Crestone End of Life Project in Colorado, Agus Lamba and Katie Innamorato in Indonesia, Claudia Tapia and Mayra Cisneros in Mexico, Eriko Takeuchi and Ayako Sato in Japan, Katrina Spade and Cheryl Johnston in North Carolina, Jordi Nadal in Spain, and Andres Bedoya in Bolivia.

Finally Landis Blair, who was an all-right boyfriend but is now a killer collaborator.

SOURCES

Introduction

Fraser, James W. *Cremation: Is It Christian?* Loizeaux Brothers, Inc., 1965.

Herodotus. *The History.* Translated by David Grene, University of Chicago Press, 2010.

Seeman, Erik R. *Death in the New World: Cross-Cultural Encounters, 1492–1800.* University of Pennsylvania Press, 2011.

———. *The Huron–Wendat Feast of the Dead: Indian–European Encounters in Early North America.* Johns Hopkins University Press, 2011.

Colorado

Abbey, Edward. *Desert Solitaire: A Season in the Wilderness.* Ballantine Books, 1971.

"Hindu Fights for Pyre 'Dignity.'" BBC News, March 24, 2009.

Johanson, Mark. "Mungo Man: The Story Behind the Bones that Forever Changed Australia's History." *International Business Times,* March 4, 2014.

Kapoor, Desh. "Last Rites of Deceased in Hinduism." *Patheos,* January 2, 2010.

Laungani, Pittu. "Death in a Hindu Family." *Death and Bereavement Across Cultures.* Edited by Colin Murray Parkes, Pittu Laungani, and Bill Young. Taylor & Francis, Inc., 1997.

Marsh, Michael. "Newcastle Hindu Healer Babaji Davender Ghai Reignites Funeral Pyre Plans." *Chronicle Live,* February 1, 2015.

Mayne Correia, Pamela M. "Fire Modification of Bone: A Review of the Literature." In *Forensic Taphonomy: The Postmortem Fate of Human Remains.* Edited by Marcella H. Sorg and William D. Haglund. CRC Press, 1996.

Prothero, Stephen. *Purified by Fire: A History of Cremation in America.* University of California Press, 2002.

Savage, David G. "Monks in Louisiana Win Right to Sell Handcrafted Caskets." *Los Angeles Times,* October 19, 2013.

Indonesia

Adams, Kathleen M. *Art as Politics: Recrafting Identities, Tourism, and Power in Tana Toraja, Indonesia.* University of Hawaii Press, 2006.

——— "Club Dead, Not Club Med: Staging Death in Contemporary Tana Toraja (Indonesia)." *Southeast Asian Journal of Social Science* 21, no. 2 (1993): 62–72.

——— "Ethnic Tourism and the Renegotiation of Tradition in Tana Toraja (Sulawesi, Indonesia)." *Ethnology* 36, no. 4 (1997): 309–20.

Chambert-Loir, Henri, and Anthony Reid, eds. *The Potent Dead: Ancestors, Saints and Heroes in Contemporary Indonesia.* University of Hawaii Press, 2002.

Mitford, Jessica. *The American Way of Death Revisited.* Knopf Doubleday, 2011.

Tsintjilonis, Dimitri. "The Death-Bearing Senses in Tana Toraja." *Ethnos* 72, no. 2 (2007): 173–94.

Volkman, Toby. "The Riches of the Undertaker." *Indonesia* 28 (1979): 1–16.

Yamashita, Shinji. "Manipulating Ethnic Tradition: The Funeral Ceremony, Tourism, and Television among the Toraja of Sulawesi." *Indonesia* 58 (1994): 69–82.

Mexico

Bradbury, Ray. "Drunk, and in Charge of a Bicycle." *The Stories of Ray Bradbury.* Alfred A. Knopf, 1980.

Carmichael, Elizabeth, and Chloë Sayer. *The Skeleton at the Feast: The Day of the Dead in Mexico.* University of Texas Press, 1991.

"Chavez Ravine: A Los Angeles Story." Written and directed by Jordan Mechner. *Independent Lens,* PBS, 2003.

The Life and Times of Frida Kahlo. Written and directed by Amy Stechler. PBS, 2005.

Lomnitz, Claudio. *Death and the Idea of Mexico.* Zone Books, 2008.

Quigley, Christine. *Modern Mummies: The Preservation of the Human Body in the Twentieth Century.* McFarland, 2006.

Zetterman, Eva. "Frida Kahlo's Abortions: With Reflections from a Gender Perspective on Sexual Education in Mexico." *Konsthistorisk Tidskrift / Journal of Art History* 75, no. 4: 230–43.

North Carolina

Brunetti, Ludovico. *Cremazione e conservazione dei cadaveri.* Translated by Ivan Cenzi. Tipografia del Seminario, 1884.

Ellis, Richard. *Singing Whales and Flying Squid: The Discovery of Marine Life.* Lyons Press, 2006.

Fryling, Kevin. "IU School of Medicine–Northwest Honors Men and Women Who Donate Their Bodies to Educate the Next Generation of Physicians." *Inside IU,* February 6, 2013.

Helliker, Kevin. "Giving Back an Identity to Donated Cadavers." *Wall Street Journal,* February 1, 2011.

Laqueur, Thomas. *The Work of the Dead: A Cultural History of Mortal Remains.* Princeton University Press, 2015.

Monbiot, George. "Why Whale Poo Matters." *Guardian,* December 12, 2014.

Nicol, Steve. "Vital Giants: Why Living Seas Need Whales." *New Scientist,* July 6, 2011.

Perrin, W. F., B. Wursig, and J. G. M. Thewissen, eds. *Encyclopedia of Marine Mammals.* Academic Press, 2002.

Pimentel, D., et al. "Environmental and Economic Costs of Soil Erosion and Conservation Benefits." *Science* 267, no. 24 (1995): 1117–22.

Rocha, Robert C., Phillip J. Clapham, and Yulia V. Ivashchenk. "Emptying the Oceans: A Summary of Industrial Whaling Catches in the 20th Century." *Marine*

Fisheries Review 76 (2014): 37–48.

Whitman, Walt. *Leaves of Grass.* Dover, 2007.

Spain

Adam, David. "Can Unburied Corpses Spread Disease?" *Guardian,* January 6, 2005.

Estrin, Daniel. "Berlin's Graveyards Are Being Converted for Use by the Living." *The World,* PRI, August 8, 2016.

Kokayeff, Nina. "Dying to Be Discovered: Miasma vs. Germ Theory." *ESSAI* 10, article 24 (2013).

Marsh, Tanya. "Home Funerals, Rent-Seeking, and Religious Liberty." *Huffington Post,* February 22, 2016.

Rahman, Rema. "Who, What, Why: What Are the Burial Customs in Islam?" BBC News, October 25, 2011.

Japan

Ashton, John, and Tom Whyte. *The Quest for Paradise.* HarperCollins, 2001.

Bernstein, Andrew. *Modern Passing: Death Rites, Politics, and Social Change in Imperial Japan.* University of Hawaii Press, 2006.

Brodesser-Akner, Taffy. "Marie Kondo and the Ruthless War on Stuff." *New York Times Magazine,* July 6, 2016.

"Family of Dead '111-Year-Old' Man Told Police He Was a 'Human Vegetable.' " *Mainchi Shimbun,* July 30, 2010.

Iga, Mamoru. *The Thorn in the Chrysanthemum: Suicide and Economic Success in Modern Japan.* University of California Press, 1986.

Lloyd Parry, Richard. *People Who Eat Darkness: The True Story of a Young Woman Who Vanished from the Streets of Tokyo — and the Evil That Swallowed Her Up.* Farrar, Straus & Giroux, 2011.

Lynn, Marri. "Thomas Willson's Metropolitan Sepulchre." *Wonders and Marvels,* 2012.

Mochizuki, Takashi, and Eric Pfanner. "In Japan, Dog Owners Feel Abandoned as Sony Stops Supporting 'Aibo.' " *Wall Street Journal,* February 11, 2015.

Schlesinger, Jacob M., and Alexander Martin. "Graying Japan Tries to Embrace the Golden Years." *Wall Street Journal,* November 29, 2015.

Stevens Curl, James. *The Egyptian Revival: Ancient Egypt as the Inspiration for Design Motifs in the West.* Routledge, 2013.

Suzuki, Hikaru. *The Price of Death: The Funeral Industry in Contemporary Japan.* Stanford University Press, 2002.

Venema, Vibeke. "How the Selfie Stick was Invented Twice." BBC World Service, April 19, 2015.

Bolivia

Dear, Paula. "The Rise of the 'Cholitas.' " BBC News, February 20, 2014.

Faure, Bernard. *The Power of Denial: Buddhism, Purity, and Gender.* Princeton University Press, 2003.

Fernández Juárez, Gerardo. "The Revolt of the 'Ñatitas': 'Ritual Empowerment' and Cycle of the Dead in La Paz, Bolivia." *Revista de Dialectología y Tradiciones Populares* 65, no. 1 (2010): 185–214.

Harper, Elizabeth. "The Neapolitan Cult of the Dead: A Profile for Virginia Commonwealth University." Virginia Commonwealth University's World Religions and Spirituality Project.

Nuwer, Rachel. "Meet the Celebrity Skulls of Bolivia's Fiesta de las Ñatitas." *Smithsonian,* November 17, 2015.

Scotto di Santolo, A., L. Evangelista, and A. Evangelista. "The Fontanelle Cemetery: Between Legend and Reality." Paper delivered at the Second International Symposium on Geotechnical Engineering for the Preservation of Monuments and Historic Sites, University of Naples Federico II.

Shahriari, Sara. "Cholitas Paceñas: Bolivia's Indigenous Women Flaunt Their Ethnic Pride." *Guardian,* April 22, 2015.

———. "Skulls and Souls: Bolivian Believers Look to the Spirit World." Al Jazeera, November 12, 2014.

Wilson, Liz. *Charming Cadavers: Horrific Figurations of the Feminine in Indian Buddhist Hagiographic Literature.* University of Chicago Press, 2006.

California

Desai, Sapur F. *History of the Bombay Parsi Punchayet, 1860–1960.* Trustees of the Parsi Punchayet Funds and Properties, 1977.

Moss, Marissa R. "Flashback: Gram Parsons Dies in the Desert." *Rolling Stone,* September 19, 2014.

Hannon, Elliot. "Vanishing Vultures a Grave Matter for India's Parsis." NPR, September 5, 2012.

Jacobi, Keith P. "Body Disposition in Cross-

Cultural Context: Prehistoric and Modern
Non-Western Societies." In *Handbook of
Death and Dying,* edited by Clifton D.
Bryant. SAGE Reference, 2003.

Kerr, Blake. *Sky Burial: An Eyewitness Account of China's Brutal Crackdown in Tibet.*
Shambhala, 1997.

Khan, Uzra. "Waiting for Vultures." *Yale
Globalist,* December 1, 2010.

Kreyenbroek, Philip G. *Living Zoroastrianism: Urban Parsis Speak about their Religion.* Routledge, 2001.

"The Strange Tale of Gram Parsons' Funeral in Joshua Tree." *DesertUSA,* September 14, 2015.

Subramanian, Meera. "India's Vanishing
Vultures." *VQR* 87 (September 9, 2015).

Epilogue

Hagerty, James R. "Funeral Industry Seeks
Ways to Stay Relevant." *Wall Street Journal,* November 3, 2016.

Ruggeri, Amanda. "The Strange, Gruesome
Truth about Plague Pits and the Tube."
BBC, September 6, 2015.

Additional Around the World Death Reading

Jones, Barbara. *Design for Death.* Bobbs-Merrill, 1967.

Koudounaris, Paul. *Memento Mori: The Dead Among Us.* Thames & Hudson, 2015.

Metcalf, Peter, and Richard Huntington. *Celebrations of Death: The Anthropology of Mortuary Ritual.* Cambridge University Press, 1991.

Murray, Sarah. *Making an Exit: From the Magnificent to the Macabre — How We Dignify the Dead.* Picador, 2012.

ABOUT THE AUTHOR

Mortician **Caitlin Doughty** — host and creator of "Ask a Mortician" and the *New York Times* best-selling author of *Smoke Gets in Your Eyes* — founded The Order of the Good Death. She lives in Los Angeles, where she runs her nonprofit funeral home, Undertaking LA.

31901062575636